To Keeley

He is worthy of the best of all you are!

EXTRAVAGANT

When Worship Becomes Lifestyle

Be Blessed

Dr John Andrews

RIVER
PUBLISHING

River Publishing & Media Ltd
Bradbourne Stables
East Malling
Kent ME19 6DZ
United Kingdom

info@river-publishing.co.uk

ISBN 978-1-908393-65-4
Cover design by www.spiffingcovers.com
Printed in the United Kingdom

Contents

Dedication

To my amazing family:
Over this last year we have walked together through the
"valley of the shadow", yet you have continued to love, serve
and give extravagantly. Few will understand the cost,
but the Lord delights in your perfume.
Thank you.

"... He blesses the home of the righteous."

Acknowledgements

Nothing of worth just happens, nor is it the product of the work of just one person. The people around me make me look much better than I am and help me to be the best I can be.

First, thanks go to Dawn. You are my *ezer*, my *anam cara* and I cannot imagine my life or this journey without you. You are worth "far more than rubies" to me and you are a gift from the Lord for which I will be eternally grateful. I love you with all my heart.

To my children, whose patience allows me to focus and finish.

To Tim Pettingale for (again) expertly helping me to get a book into print and to River Publishing for taking the risk in putting their name to mine.

Finally, to my Heavenly Father. Your extravagance has changed my past, my present and my future. I would be nothing and nowhere without your generous grace and tender mercy. Your love endures forever and that is the only reason I am still here. May the perfume of my life always please You.

Foreword

I first met John in the little village of Havercroft, Yorkshire, during his first full-time post in ministry. One would have presumed that with the size of John's gifting and potential a large metropolis would have been his natural setting, but it was in this modest setting, with an original congregation of four people (yes four!), that extravagance shone! During the time that I served with him on a summer pastorate, I watched a man pour out God's love into the hearts of a growing congregation and into the life of his village with abandonment. There were no TV crews, paparazzi or journalists filming the endless conversations, private studies and personal sacrifice. However, heaven was smiling as John broke his life over the feet of a community, filling the local area with the new fragrance of heaven.

We are almost scared to say the word "recession" these days, in case it inadvertently sparks a downward spiral in the financial markets. After the heartbreak of the Global Crisis almost eight years ago the general public have been much more circumspect in their display of any regained wealth or recovered affluence; any sense of the ostentatious is frowned upon outside the world of oligarchs and the overpaid. However, the world of worship has only one currency that never devalues and it's called *extravagance*. The book you have in your hands describes how a woman of questionable character understood eternal markets and the value of extravagance, while all her critics traded in worthless, judgmental religion. I live and pastor in the great state of California and, yes, we've got our fair share of bling and botox – but it's also refreshing to see quite literally thousands of people in a local community embrace their brokenness and throw themselves at the feet of Jesus. It's over 2000 years later and worship still works! Get ready to start an emotional journey that will be highly informative, deeply challenging, and life transforming. Your inner Pharisee is bound to be offended too!

From those humble days in Yorkshire, John's life has soared to many remarkable heights, but the guy remains the same – an extravagant worshipper. In these pages John's academic brilliance is clearly evident, his love for Scripture even more so, but it's in his everyday life that you always pick up that refreshing scent of a life lived on the edge of Extravagance.

Simply put, when you tackle a subject like extravagance it must be reflected in a lifestyle, and that reflection is crystal clear in the author. His extravagant spirit pervades his marriage, inspires his kids, reaches local communities, cares for the world and is about to impact you!

Andrew McCourt
Senior Pastor, Bayside Church, Granite Bay, California

Preface

LUKE 7:36-50

As I approach the writing of this book, I do so with both great excitement and a little apprehension. I'm excited because the material at its heart – namely, the expression of worship to the Lord through an extravagant lifestyle for the Lord – has been my core ambition for a very long time. Like so many of you, I love to sing and raise my hands in corporate worship with the called-out community of Jesus, His Church. I have had the joy of lifting my voice to Him in rooms containing only a few, as well as many thousands.

But as much as I love all of this, I am persuaded that some of our most powerful expressions of worship can, and should be, demonstrated in the ordinary, routine and, dare I say it, mundane moments of life. In the story we're about to journey through together there are no lights or bands; there's no atmosphere of faith or platform of encouragement to inspire or provoke the woman at the centre of the action – there's just an opportunity to do something for Jesus, to show Him how much He's loved, and to express to Him how grateful she is!

My apprehension resides in the fact that three people I have come to know and love for different reasons collide in this mesmerising episode.

The first is Dr Luke. He's the only Gentile contributor to the New Testament, yet he captures so brilliantly the Jewishness of Jesus, while at the same time connecting Him to a Gentile world that knows little of His story and His people. As is so typical of Luke, Jesus is not only sharing food, He's sharing His life, at ease with the religious while, at the same time, embracing the marginalised of His world. The unique stories of Luke, of which this is one, have so often at their core the Saviour who has come to *"seek and save the lost"*.[1] Luke's Jesus is prepared to leave the many for the one, moving from the centre to the fringe, and is willing to dismantle man-made tradition-fences if they prevent the lost from being found.[2] In the worldview of Dr Luke, Jesus has come to proclaim favour not vengeance; He's come to call and not condemn, through a message of salvation and status reversal.

The second is the woman. My wife, Dawn, can testify to the fact that I have lived with this woman for a very long time. If I could hitch a ride in Doctor Who's Tardis, this event would be on my time travel bucket list. We're not absolutely sure of her background and we're sketchy as to what happens next, but what we are sure of is that for a few glorious moments this unnamed woman demonstrates the heart of the Torah through the humility of her audacity, the authenticity of her generosity, and the purity of her passion.

As we shall see, she is totally silent, yet our ears ring with the sound of her offering. Though her actions look spontaneous, the text makes it clear that this was no accidental fluke; everything was intentional on her part. Most in the room may have been offended by her behaviour, but heaven saw it as pure. She was not looking for applause from men, rather she was seeking an opportunity to serve the Lord. Her outrageous extravagance divided the room, but brought great delight to the heart of Jesus. Having lived with this woman for so long, I have taken it upon myself to bring her story afresh to a generation that will benefit from hearing her voice. I only pray that my words will do her extravagance justice.

The third person, of course, is Jesus. I encountered Jesus for the first time by revelation and faith when I was eight years old. I was sitting on the end seat, a few rows from the front, in a children's service in Mayo Street City Mission, just off the Shankhill Road in Belfast. As I listened to the preacher, I had a picture of Jesus standing at my heart's door, asking to come in. Without any emotion or even an appeal, I turned to my friend and said, "Tonight I'm going to become a Christian," and I did!

That night I knew Jesus was the Son of God, a truth I have never doubted or questioned from that day to this. In the years that have followed, I have come to know Jesus as my Saviour, my Teacher and my Lord. In knowing Him, my love for Him has deepened and strengthened. I cannot imagine my life without Him and there is nothing in the world I want to do, other than serve Him. Like Thomas I confess, "My Lord and my God."[3]

Though much of our focus will be on the actions of the woman, we must not forget the reason for her actions. She was extravagant to Jesus because He had been extravagant to her. What we see from her is only a reflection of what He had done in her and for her. The smell of expensive perfume filled the room because the glory of His love had transformed her heart. If you read this book and see only the woman (as amazing as she is), I will have failed completely. For in truth, this story is not about her, but about Him. If we understand what He has done for us, extravagance will become normal, not exceptional.

If we remember what we were before He entered our world and who we are now because of His grace, we will conclude that whatever we offer to Him, no matter how generous it may seem, is still a bargain compared to the "indescribable gift" we have received.

The dictionary describes extravagance as, "passing the bounds of reason, wild, absurd, flamboyant, abundant or even wasteful". These words may well describe the actions of this woman, but as I look at God's salvation story, and the lengths to which He was prepared to go to in order to save His world, *extravagant* perhaps begins to describe it. When I think of Jesus, God in flesh, coming into the world, full of grace and truth and giving His life so extravagantly for me, for us, on the cross, though I know the details, my mind cannot comprehend the dimensions of His love. In praying for the church at Ephesus, Paul writes:

> "And I pray that you, being rooted and established in love, may have the power, together with all the saints, to grasp how wide and long and high and deep is the love of Christ, and to know this love that surpasses knowledge – that you may be filled to the measure of all the fulness of God."[4]

I really do love how the Message puts this:

> "And I ask Him that with both feet planted firmly on love, you'll be able to take in with all Christians the *extravagant dimensions of Christ's love.*"[5]

We only struggle with extravagance *for* the Lord when we lose sight of the extravagance *of* the Lord. Giving is never an issue when we comprehend how much we have been forgiven.

As you read and meditate on the message of this book, I pray that you will be inspired by the extravagance of the woman as we shed light on the power of her actions and the cost of her gift. But I also pray that you will be captivated afresh with who Jesus is and what He has done for you. When we grasp that we have been forgiven much, extravagant love will generously flow. When we understand that we have freely received, an extravagant lifestyle will naturally follow.

May you know the power of His extravagant love and may the world experience the perfume of your extravagant worship!

Dr John Andrews
September 2016

Endnotes
1. Luke 19:10
2. Jesus teaching in Luke 15 is a great example of this
3. John 20:28
4. Ephesians 3:17-19
5. My italics

Chapter 1 – Time Travellers

Before we delve into the rich tapestry of this story, it is important to take a moment to reflect on where it came from and how it arrived. This is not a random event that has stumbled into Dr Luke's narrative. Rather, this is a jewel unearthed by the doctor's meticulous research and helped by the Holy Spirit. It shines gloriously in the diadem of his unique stories. Luke has a message he's desperate to tell, and the events that transpired that evening in the house of Simon the Pharisee conspire to help his cause.

Though this story sounds similar to another one contained in the other Gospels, it is important to recognise that it is, in fact, unique. Like all the Gospel writers, Luke clearly draws on some information common to all, weaving elements of this shared information into his own particular Spirit-inspired agenda. However, Luke also presents a whole body of material around Jesus that is totally unique. After "...carefully investigating everything from the beginning..." his "orderly account" enriches the story of Jesus, whilst also enhancing the person of Jesus.[1]

In Matthew 26:6-13, Mark 14:3-9 and John 12:1-8, we also have a story of a woman anointing Jesus, but when compared to our story in Luke 7:36-50, there are some noticeable differences which convince us that the two events are similar, but ultimately very different.

Let me highlight the key differences.

In Luke, Jesus is in the house of Simon the pharisee in the north of the country, whereas in Matthew, Mark and John He's in the house of Simon the leper, located in Bethany in the south.

In Luke the anointing takes place in the early part of Jesus' ministry, whereas in the other accounts it happens towards the end of Jesus' ministry, just before His death.

In Luke the woman is unnamed, whereas John tells us it was Mary, the sister of Martha and Lazarus, who anoints Jesus.

In Luke, Jesus is alone, but in Bethany His disciples are with Him as witnesses.

In Luke, Simon is the one offended by the woman's actions, whereas in the other accounts it is some of the disciples in general and Judas in particular who become offended. In fact, Matthew makes it clear that the experience of being rebuked by Jesus was a tipping point for Judas to agree to betray Him.[2]

Finally, in Luke, the woman's actions are those of praise, thanksgiving and surrender, whereas the woman in Matthew, Mark and John is clearly preparing Jesus for His burial.

Why is this important?

With the story of the anointing at Bethany already in circulation, it would have been easy for Luke to leave this event on the shelf along with his other research scrolls. But the fact that he includes it in his narrative, despite the possible confusion that might arise as a result, represents his conviction in the message at the heart of this story and the truths brought to the light through the encounter this woman has with Jesus. If we let them speak, Luke has something to tell us and the woman has something to teach us. I'm glad Luke took the risk! It is important when dealing with any passage in the Scriptures to place them first in their context. When we can hear and understand the message in its original setting, we have a chance of applying it to our current setting. If we can grasp the story in the context in which it was written, we can allow it to speak with authority into the context in which it is read. As Shillington puts it, "Texts do not yield interpretive fruit when plucked from the native soil in which they were rooted."[3]

To help us enjoy the fruit of this particular tree we need to understand some key components of the "native soil" in which it was rooted.

Meals and mayhem
"…He went to the Pharisee's house and reclined at the table." (Luke 7:36)

I love how Karris puts it: "In Luke's Gospel Jesus is either going to a meal, at a meal, or coming from a meal. In Luke's Gospel Jesus got Himself killed because of the way He ate."[4]

I'm not sure I'd go that far, but I love the spirit of what he's trying to capture. In the culture of Jesus, eating in someone's house or sharing your table with others was always about more than food. To welcome people at the table had become tantamount to extending to them intimacy, solidarity and acceptance. Table companions were treated as though they were extended family and sharing food carried encoded messages about hierarchy, inclusion and exclusion, boundaries and crossing boundaries. "Who ate with whom at table, where one sat in relation to whom at table – such questions were charged with social meaning in the time of Jesus and Luke."[5]

For sure, Jesus always seems to be eating in Luke. If we

exclude the meals with His disciples, there are six recorded meals throughout the Gospel and all of them are interesting. The perception of many is that Jesus only really had dinner with sinners, but when we consider the Lukan evidence closely, we see an interesting split.

Jesus shared three meals in the houses of Pharisees:

- Luke 7... our story
- Luke 11:37-52
- Luke 14:1-24

He also shared three meals in the homes of "sinners":

- Luke 5:29-32
- Luke 15:1-2 (3-32)
- Luke 19:1-10

Of these six meals, all are unique to Luke with the exception of the story of Levi (Matthew) in Luke 5.

Why is this important to understanding our story?

Firstly, Jesus was as comfortable in the house of a sinner as he was in the house of the religious. The fact that we have an even split of where He ate, shows us He did not reject the religious in favour of the sinner, nor abandon an invitation offered to Him, regardless of who made the offer, or why.

Secondly, every meal became the means of a message. Some of the most powerful statements and teaching of Jesus are given to us over or around a meal. If you will take the time to examine the words of Jesus around food in Luke's Gospel alone, you'll be amazed at what was on the menu. In Jesus' world, food was never only about food – it opened the door to fellowship, debate, sharing and learning ... and Jesus took full advantage of the offer, every time!

Thirdly, every one of the six meals I've referenced in Luke concluded in controversy. I won't go into detail on our story now, as this will be dealt with later in the book, but let me summarise the rest for you:

- **Luke 5** – Jesus was asked why He shared the table with tax collectors and sinners. He replied: "I have not come to call the righteous, but sinners to repentance." (v32)
- **Luke 11** – Jesus launched into six woes specifically aimed at the Pharisaic community and He certainly did not pull any punches. It's interesting that Jesus reserved His most aggressive language for those, who as far as God's Law was concerned, should have known better! The meal didn't end well. "When Jesus left there, the Pharisees and the teachers of the law began to oppose Him fiercely and to besiege Him with questions, waiting to catch Him in something He might say." (v53-54)
- **Luke 14** – At the house of a "prominent Pharisee" Jesus in no uncertain terms challenges His listeners about their attitudes, through the healing of the man with dropsy, by reminding them "…everyone who exalts himself will be humbled, and he who humbles himself will be exalted" (v11). He went on to suggest that His esteemed audience may not get the places they expect at the great feast of the Kingdom of God. If they are not careful, their seats might be given to the "poor, the crippled, the blind and the lame" instead! (v21)
- **Luke 15** – At this meal, Jesus is surrounded by sinners while the Pharisees and teachers of the law populate the fringe of the gathering. Surely the irony of this moment was not lost on Jesus as a physical metaphor of the "status reversal" His Kingdom was ushering in. When seen against this backdrop, His climatic parable of the "Lost Sons" becomes

even more powerful and controversial, as the "pig-smelling" son is welcomed in while the self-righteous son misses the party!

- **Luke 19** – Jesus invites Himself to the house of the "chief tax collector" and, over dinner, revolutionizes Zacchaeus' life. As a result of this encounter Zacchaeus demonstrated he had truly repented by making restitution and restoration for the wrongs he had done and by the end of the story is called a "son of Abraham". That's where most people leave the story, but Jesus continued His teaching with the parable of the Ten Minas, the meaning of which is frighteningly simple. If we humble ourselves to the Lord's rulership, and take care of what God has given us, more will be added. But if we don't, what we have will be taken away. Though once excluded, Zacchaeus is now included – thus Jesus warns those who believe themselves to be included to be careful lest they be excluded!

In every meal that Jesus showed up at, mayhem ensued. Why would the meal at Simon's house be any different?

Religion and rules

"Be on your guard against the yeast of the Pharisees, which is hypocrisy." (Luke 12:1)

The word hypocrite is used 18 times in the Gospels, but in each case, is used only by Jesus.[6] Of those 18 times, 15 are directed at or around the religious community. This creates the impression that Jesus didn't like the religious, but as we've seen previously, the statistics from Luke's account show that Jesus was willing to eat with the religious as much as He was with the sinners.

The word hypocrite, *hypokritēs* is made up of two words,

from *hypo*, under and *krínō*, to judge, carrying with it the idea of *judging under*, like a performer acting *under a mask* and pointing figuratively to the concept of being a *two-faced* person. Jesus saw the "yeast of the Pharisees" as their pretense expressed in their willingness to live a life of two-faces, in order to maintain their position before the people, thus impressing them with external things – regardless of the condition of their internal world.

Though the word hypocrite does not appear in the Hebrew Bible, some words carry a similar idea. For example,

> "The Lord detests those whose hearts are *perverse*, but He delights in those whose ways are *blameless*." (Proverbs 11:20)

The contrast in the verse is seen in the words *perverse* (*iqqesh*) עִקֵּשׁ – meaning twisted, deceitful, lacking genuine truth, and *blameless* (*tamim*) תָּמִים – meaning complete, whole, entire and sound. When we live perversely, people get what we want them to see, but when we walk blamelessly, people get to see what we truly are!

Ironically, this is at the heart of a question about taxes, brought to Jesus when He was teaching in the Temple.[7]

> "Teacher we know you are a man of integrity and that you teach the way of God in accordance with the truth. You aren't swayed by men, because you pay no attention to who they are." (Matthew 22:16)

The opponents of Jesus pre-fixed their question in verse 17 with this statement, in which they declare Jesus to be *blameless* – that is, His life and words match and they are, in fact, one and the same. How authentic their words were at this moment is a matter of debate, but nonetheless, they are remarkable. Their conclusion is striking:

"You aren't swayed by men, because you pay no attention to who they are."

A more literal translation of this statement might read, "You do not look on a persons face…"

Jesus clashed with the religious community in general, and the Pharisees in particular, over areas of practice rather than specific belief. In fact, if we look closely at what the Pharisees believed and what Jesus taught, there are huge similarities, leading some to suggest that Jesus was a "charismatic Pharisee", seeking to liberate those zealous for the law, just as much as bringing life to the sinner. Most of His theological flashpoints were with the Pharisees, generally because they always seemed to be where He was. Were they hounding Him, or just harassing Him, or maybe hoping to save Him?

The presence of Jesus, therefore, at the house of Simon the Pharisee should not come as a shock to us. Whatever Simon's motives were in inviting Jesus to dine, I believe He accepted the invitation because He loved Simon and wanted him to see what religion without masks really looked like.

Salvation and sinners

"For the Son of Man came to seek and to save that which was lost." (Luke 19:10)

"…Jesus should not be making friends with those who are not His own kind, that is, with toll collectors and sinners. Jesus' conduct is scandalous."[8] Like every society, the world of Jesus also contained the marginalised, created by race, colour, gender, material status, education and occupational differences.

What made the margins of Jesus' world even more painful to Him was the fact that some were created and endorsed by an interpretation of the Law He came to fulfill. Though Jesus never once broke the Law, He continuously challenged barriers that had been erected around God to protect and defend Him. Jesus did not come to protect God, but to proclaim Him, and in doing so, He found Himself deliberately in the margins of His world, advancing into territory that no self-respecting religious man would go. He was as comfortable in the market place as in the synagogue, and it seems the "common people heard Him gladly" because He looked like one of them. Sinners liked Jesus not because He was a sinner like them, but because He loved them.

On many occasions when defending the plight of the marginalised, Jesus contrasted them to someone regarded as being "safe in the centre", blessed by God as evidenced in their wealth or position. Some of Jesus' most shocking stories invite the margins to the centre, while threatening those who believe themselves to be at the centre with divine eviction! This is seen over and over again in Luke's Gospel. Here are some examples.

The widow and the captain – Luke 4:14-30
Jesus holds up a Gentile widow's faith in the time of Elijah, in contrast to the numerous widows in Israel; and a Syrian captain's obedience during the ministry of Elisha in contrast to the many lepers in Israel. These two stories almost got Him killed!

The Samaritan and the Priest/Levite – Luke 10:25-37
Interestingly, Jesus never refers to the Samaritan as "good", it's the translators who do that. But the Samaritan is the hero neighbour, in contrast to the two men of God who pass by.

The Feast of the Kingdom – Luke 14:15-24
Jesus dared to suggest that the broken would get to the table before the "blessed".

The younger and elder son – Luke 15:11-32
The younger "pig-smelling" brother got to dance at the party, while the elder "self-righteous" brother sulked outside. His unwillingness to accept his previously marginalised brother created the barrier for his own exclusion.

The rich man and Lazarus – Luke 16:19-31
Though the dogs licked Lazarus' sores, he is the one by Abraham's side, while the wealthy "God-blessed" man found himself in torment, separated from the congregation of the righteous.

The pharisee and the tax collector – Luke 18:9-14
When the pharisee prayed in the Temple, his eloquent prayer was heard only by him, while the stumbling words of the tax collector were not only heard, but ensured he went away justified.

The poor widow – Luke 21:1-4
Having probably given one of the smallest offerings of the day, the widow is declared the most generous of all. Unnoticed by her world, she is celebrated by the Lord.

Jesus' passion for the margins is also demonstrated within Luke's Gospel in His commitment to the sick. "To be sick was to be an outcast",[9] carrying with it the double edge of the potential incapacity and poverty that often accompanied illness, and the belief that sickness may well be the judgment of God, an outward sign of inner sin. Dr Luke records four unique healing stories in his account, which powerfully demonstrate the courage of Jesus as He reached out to the untouchable margins of His world.

The raising of the widow's son – Luke 7:11-17

It is so easy to miss the uniquely powerful moment in this story. Our eyes tend to be drawn to the raising of the boy, and why not. But if we focus there we'll miss the reason for the miracle. The text tells us, "… and Jesus gave him back to his mother" (v15). Jesus didn't heal the boy because he was dead; rather he raised the boy because without him, the widow would have been completely destitute and therefore marginalised. In raising the boy he saved her from the margins. I love the tenderness of Jesus to the woman, perhaps mindful of His own mother, herself a widow!

The healing of the woman bent double – Luke 13:10-17 (18-21)

As Jesus taught that day, a woman appeared in the synagogue, catching His eye. She had suffered for eighteen years, carrying not only the burden of sickness, but the stigma of a sinner. Perhaps she turned up that day to hear the young Rabbi speak, hopeful that His message would be different from the mantra she had become so accustomed to. Jesus called her forward, spoke to her, touched her and healed her. If that wasn't enough, He then defended her and finally announced her to be a "daughter of Abraham", the only place in the whole of the Bible where a woman is given this title!

The man with dropsy – Luke 14:1-6 (7-24)

Similar to the story of Luke 13, this healing takes place on a Sabbath, in the house of a prominent pharisee, and like the woman, Jesus contrasts the fate of this suffering man to that of an animal (in this case an ox that falls into a well). If the ox can be rescued on the Sabbath, then why not this man? Jesus not only healed the man, but He elevated him, opening up the way for him to return to his world, whole and free.

The ten lepers – Luke 17:11-19

The border between Samaria and Galilee "housed" the leper colony of Jesus' day. On His way down to Jerusalem, Jesus travelled along the border and was met by ten lepers. A casual reading of this text suggests this was all a coincidence, but a closer look shows us that Jesus deliberately entered the world of the leper, because He wanted to meet them. It would have been a miracle for Jesus not to "bump into" lepers. All ten are healed (cleansed), but only one returns to give thanks, a Samaritan, and he is not only cleansed by Jesus, but proclaimed whole through his faith.

When we observe the events in Simon's house and set them in the context of the big picture of Luke's Gospel, it all makes perfect sense. Though culturally and religiously shocking, we now understand the reaction of Jesus, His irritation at Simon's attitude, and His tender generosity to the woman. What we are given the privilege to observe is a glorious microcosm of the mission of Jesus, to reach out to the margins and welcome the sinners.

Messiah and misunderstanding

"Are you the one who is to come, or should we expect someone else?" (Luke 7:19-20)

These words were uttered by the greatest prophet that ever lived – the one given the responsibility of being the harbinger for the Messiah. John knew who he was and what his purpose was and I believe he also understood that Jesus was the Messiah, as seen at the baptism of Jesus. However, John found himself in prison because he personally criticised Herod for taking his brother's wife. It's while in prison that John sends his disciples to ask Jesus this remarkable question. Some have suggested that John's question is a crisis of faith, a reflection of his own imprisonment, or an expression of impatience at Jesus' unwillingness to help his plight. However, I think John's question is an indication of his own expectation of what the Messiah, *his* Messiah, would look like. When John was preaching he declared,

> "I baptize you with water. But one more powerful than I will come, the thongs of whose sandals I am not worthy to untie. He will baptize you with the Holy Spirit and fire. His winnowing fork is in his hand to clear his threshing floor and to gather the wheat into his barn, but he will burn up the chaff with unquenchable fire." (Luke 3:16-17)

Note the references to judgment in John's words. The fire he refers to is not the purifying fire of the Spirit, but rather of the vengeance and judgement of God, who in saving His people, will also judge and condemn His enemies – a very popular idea among many of that day. John's salvation included the fire of judgement and he fully expected his Messiah to get his fork out and go to work! However, the reports he heard of Jesus didn't contain fire, but rather inclusion and acceptance. When announcing His mission at His home synagogue, Jesus quoted Isaiah 61, but stopped short at proclaiming the "day of vengeance of our God" and instead heralded in the "year of God's favour".[10] Without explicitly saying it, Jesus was correcting the perception of His harbinger, and letting the world know that although fire would eventually come, that wasn't what He had come to bring.

It is interesting that when Jesus sent John's disciples back, He asked them to relay to John "what they have seen and heard":

"The blind receive sight, the lame walk, those who have leprosy are cured, the deaf hear, the dead are raised, and the good news is preached to the poor." (v22)

These words are remarkably similar to those Jesus quotes from Isaiah 61. It seems Jesus was proclaiming favour, not fire!

Jesus' conclusion on the matter is unmistakable:

"Blessed is the man who does not fall away on account of me." (v23)

Though Jesus may not have been what John hoped Him to be, Jesus' hope was that John would not lose faith in the Messiah He was. John prepared the way for others, now Jesus is urging John not to lose the way himself.

Could it be a coincidence that John's question comes immediately before the story of the woman in Luke's account? Or that, maybe, just maybe, Dr Luke intentionally arranged his material in this order, so that the message released in the fragrance of her perfume served to demonstrate what sort of Messiah had come among us – the friend of sinners, bringing favour and not fire! Perhaps, like John, Simon looked at Jesus that night and stumbled, concluding, "He cannot be the One."

But just as Jesus challenged John, so Simon is challenged, to move beyond the boundaries set by his own expectations and see the Saviour who reclines before him.

Chapter seven begins with a Roman centurion understanding that Jesus is God's Messiah, commended by Jesus with the words:

"I tell you, I have not found such great faith even in Israel." (Luke 7:9)

It ends with Jesus being lavishly and extravagantly anointed by a "sinful woman" of whom Jesus declares,

"Your faith has saved you; go in peace." (Luke 7:50)

In the heart of the chapter, we have a prophet asking a painful question: "Are you the One who was to come, or should we expect someone else?" (Luke 7:19), while a pharisee arrives at a dangerous conclusion:

"If this man were a prophet, he would know who is touching him and what kind of a woman she is – that she is a sinner." (Luke 7:39)

Both men struggled to see the One before them, stumbling over their own expectations, in danger of missing the Jesus who came to save. It seems the centurion and the woman call from the margins to the prophet and pharisee at the centre, in the hope that they will also see and not fall away on account of Him.

"But wisdom is proved right by all her children." (Luke 7:35)

Endnotes

1. Luke 1:1-4
2. Matthew 26:14. Read this in context of the previous verses
3. Shillington, V.G., *The New Testament in Context*, London: T&T Clark, 2008, p2.
4. Karris, R.J., *Eating Your Way Through Luke*, Minnesota: Liturgical

Press, 2006, p97.

5. Green, J.B., *The Theology of the Gospel of Luke*, Cambridge: Cambridge University Press, 1995, p87.

6. Mt.6:2, 5, 16, 7:5, 15:7, 22:18, 23:13, 14, 15, 23, 25, 27, 29, 24:51, Mk.7:6, Lk.6:42, 12:56 & 13:15

7. Matthew 22:15-22

8. Karris, p27.

9. Shillington, p41.

10. Compare Isaiah 61:1-2 with Luke 4:18-19

Chapter 2 – Summoned to Serve
Extravagant Service

The room was already filled with tension before the woman stepped forward to anoint Jesus. Simon the pharisee had invited Jesus to dinner, and although a feast would be put before them, everyone knew that Jesus was the main dish on the menu. This was undoubtedly a moment to cross-examine the young Rabbi and test His theology a little bit more. Whether Simon's motives were to *save* Jesus or expose Him, a night of verbal combat awaited them all. Added to this, the narrative makes it clear that Simon, the host for the evening, had not extended to Jesus what would have been regarded at the time as basic social etiquette. Jesus was offered no water to clean His dirty feet, or scented oil to freshen His sweaty body, or even a simple kiss of greeting to welcome Him as a friend. As Jesus reclined at the table, He found Himself in the crosshairs of a curious opponent, whose finger it seemed was poised over the trigger … *and then it happened!*

"A woman in that town who lived a sinful life learned that Jesus was eating at the Pharisee's house, so she came there with an alabaster jar of perfume. As she stood behind Him at His feet weeping, she began to wet His feet with her tears.

Then she wiped them with her hair, kissed them and poured perfume on them." (v37-38)

Suddenly, all eyes were diverted from Jesus to the woman, as Simon and his guests struggled to comprehend what was happening and how they might respond to it. Jesus is, for a few moments, no longer the centre of their attention. Instead, Simon's scope wheels round and begins to focus on her. But before he can fire the first shot, before a word of denouncement or condemnation is uttered, the woman begins to do the unthinkable, making him a captive spectator to a horror show in his own home. In one dramatic moment, the woman's action *saved* Jesus and *silenced* His host and though she never says a word, her behaviour speaks loud and clear!

On the evening in question, the actions of the woman happened quickly and Dr Luke lists the four elements of her behaviour in one brief sentence containing just thirty-one words in the original language of the text. So over the next few chapters we're going to slow this sentence down, taking it frame by frame, allowing us to uncover the power of each movement and appreciating the nuance within the detail in order that, with fresh eyes, we might start to comprehend the extent of her extravagance towards Jesus. As we've seen, the dictionary describes extravagance as, "passing the bounds of reason, wild, absurd, flamboyant, abundant or even wasteful". Her actions seem to exemplify this and more and, as such, they are worthy of a few moments of our time.

Her service was Intentional
It's easy to get the impression that what happened in Simon's house was a random, spontaneous action from an "emotional"

woman, who in a moment of social and cultural irrationality had gate-crashed the party. But an examination of the text makes it clear this could not be further from the truth.

"A woman … *learned* that Jesus was eating…" (v37)

The ESV puts it:

"…when she *learned* that He was reclining…"

The word translated "learned" is **epiginōskō**, carrying the meaning literally of *upon to know*, or to *fully know*. The idea is of coming to know something, finding out, gathering the information and reaching a fact-based conclusion. The woman's "coming to know" was not an accident, but rather something she actively engaged in. Her knowledge of Jesus' whereabouts was not a coincidence. Rather, she knew where He was because she was tracking where He went!

As if to emphasise her intentionality, Luke makes it clear that she,

"…came there with an alabaster jar of perfume…" (v37)

The dictionary defines intentional as "to do on purpose, to be deliberate". There is a debate among scholars as to whether the woman intended to anoint the head of Jesus and then changed her mind, because Simon had left the feet of his guest unwashed. Whatever your conclusion on this, what we know for sure is that she turned up deliberately and she turned up ready, perfume in hand, to give her gift to Jesus.

The Lord I serve is profoundly intentional. What might look spontaneous are actions flowing out of His vision, passion and purpose. He begins with the end in mind, thus ensuring that everything He does is saturated with meaning and dripping with value. There are no afterthoughts with The Lord, only forethoughts. The Scriptures declare:

"In the beginning God created the heavens and the earth…"[1]

"The Word became flesh and made His dwelling among us..."[2]

"For God so loved the world that He gave His One and only Son..."[3]

"But when the time had fully come, God sent His Son..."[4]

"For He chose us in Him before the creation of the world..."[5]

His intentionality is one of the greatest testaments to His love for us and His attention to detail should only assure us of the magnificence of His character and depths of His loving-kindness, which the Bible declares, "endures forever".[6]

When we act without premeditation, it might be concluded that we acted spontaneously. Spontaneity sounds romantic, free and exciting, but by very definition it must also be random, erratic and unpredictable. A woman may enjoy getting a spontaneous bunch of flowers, but that might be her last for a while. A spontaneous call surprises and blesses us, but what about the long silence until the next time? Spontaneity looks great in a movie and sounds wonderful in a seminar, but, for me, *intentional* trumps spontaneous every time. In fact, I'm convinced that the more intentional and prepared I am, the more spontaneous I can be. Everything we do comes from somewhere, every action has a beginning, and all behaviour is the result of belief. What sometimes looks like spontaneity can often be intentionality at play.

One of my favourite pictures now hangs as a large canvas in our home. It dates back to 2008 when my wife, Dawn, and I visited China for the very first time to celebrate our 20th wedding anniversary. Dawn had always wanted to go to China and back in 2004 I discovered that (in British custom), china is the traditional gift for a 20th anniversary (the material, not the country). So, even though we didn't have much money, in 2004 I declared to Dawn that I would take her to China for our "china" anniversary. That gave me four years to save and plan. Helped by some God-sent blessings we made it to China in May 2008. One of the places Dawn desperately wanted to go whilst there was, of course, The Great Wall of China and we made it. As we climbed towards the Peking Tower we stopped, took in the sights, had a "how did we get here?" moment, then did something we promised ourselves we would do if we got the chance to stand on the Great Wall ... we kissed. That kiss was captured in a picture and now lives on canvas, as well as in the memories of our hearts. As we kissed, onlookers may have concluded we were two silly Westerners having a spontaneous moment of romance on one of the Wonders of the World ... but the truth is, that "spontaneous" kiss was four years in the making!

If a lifestyle of worship is left to the mercy of the spontaneous, then what should be usual will become occasional. Feelings, emotions and experiences, whether they be good, bad or ugly, will start to drive the agenda, reducing worship to a random, unpremeditated expression that creates a spiritual high for us, but little else. A truly extravagant worship-lifestyle doesn't need an excuse because it has found a cause. It's not reliant on the direction of the wind, the angle of the sun or the atmosphere of a room. It's not random, but is based on a revelation-built rationale that works out of truth, replacing *occasional* with *intentional*.

The Lord loves intentional. He honoured Abel's offering because it was the "best of the best". He sent Abraham provision because He knew Abraham truly feared Him. He let Solomon build a Temple because his father David desperately wanted to do it. It seems to me He's more interested in *why* and *how* we bring to Him, than what we bring to Him.

The woman arrived at Simon's house because Jesus was there and she brought her alabaster jar because Jesus was there. What unfolded that evening was not random or spontaneous, for such words do disservice to her extravagance. This was intentional, premeditated, and deliberately executed. He was there, so she went there. He had saved her, so she would show her gratitude to Him. His host had failed Him, so she would serve Him!

Her service was Audacious

Audacious is great word. It's one of those words that sounds right for the action it is describing. When it comes to the definition of audacious, there are two sides to the one coin. The more positive definition is "showing a willingness to take surprisingly bold risks", and there's no doubt that this fits the actions of the woman. But there's also a more negative definition which reads, "showing an impudent lack of respect", and it might be argued by Simon and his friends that this is exactly what the woman did. Though his door was open to all (we'll come to back to this later), she was certainly not welcome, and her behaviour is so shocking at multiple levels that "impudent" might have been one of the least offensive words Simon could have used to describe what she did!

So which is it? Are we looking at actions of "surprising bold risk" or "impudent disrespect"? The text is most helpful in unpacking the answer for us. Let's consider two key phrases Dr Luke uses:

"A woman in that town…" (v37)

For me, the NIV is weak here because the expression

literally reads, καὶ ἰδοὺ γυνὴ – "and look a woman". The implication being that the woman appeared in an unexpected way, surprising the gathering. The same lovely phrase is used in Luke 13:11, where a woman who has been bound by Satan for eighteen years is healed and set free, declared by Jesus to be a "daughter of Abraham". In Luke 13 it is not until Jesus is teaching that He sees the woman, suggesting either He hadn't noticed her up to that point, which considering her condition would have been improbable or, more likely, as He was teaching she appeared at the door of the synagogue: "and look a woman".

This thought has led some people to describe the actions of the woman in Luke 7 akin to that of a gate-crasher, smashing her way through social convention and acting disrepectfully to everyone in her world. After all, she had lived a life of sinful rebellion, what's a little more rebellion on the list? However, this is to misuderstand the context. Though Simon had invited specific guests to his home for dinner, there was a practice that those who had the wealth and the room to do so, would allow anyone to gather as an onlooker to the dinner party, listening to the conversations in the home, with the hope that any food left at the end would be distributed as an act of alms to the poor. For you and I this seems a bit unusual, a sort of 1st Century Big Brother, but such a context explains perfectly how a nortorious sinner could have entered Simon's house undetected and got to his chief guest so easily. She didn't gate-crash, she was "invited" if not welcome. Perhaps with head veiled she stood in the crowd, awaiting her moment to move.

But note the second phrase when considering her audacity: "And she stood behind Him at His feet weeping…" (v38)

When she eventually did make her move, note how she

behaved. She did not speak; she did not climb over the table or abuse the men present. She did not unfurl a banner or chain herself to the wall … rather she quickly and quietly moved to the one place she wanted to be. When she reached the couch where Jesus was reclining, she "stood behind Him…". She didn't walk round in front of Him, she didn't approach His face or force an unwanted confrontation, instead she assumed a position of humility and prepared to lavish extravagance on His *feet*!

Dr Luke includes this little detail because he wants us to see something about the woman and the paradox at work in her actions. Yes, she is audacious, as she moves to take a *surprising bold risk* in Simon's house, but she is not disrespectful; she's not impudent; she's trying not to embarrass the host by standing behind Jesus and ministering only to His feet. She's not on a mission to challenge the social convention of her day, but rather, all she wants to do is lavish her love on the man who has changed her world. Her audacity must not be confused with what looks like arrogance. The woman was both humble and courageous, and her audacity before men must be seen in contrast to her humility before Jesus.

When we live a lifestyle of worship, there will be moments when others will interpret *our bold risks* for the Lord as *impudent disrespect*. It can be a case of beauty being in the eye of the beholder. As it was that evening in Simon's house, sometimes it's how people see it and not what it actually is that forms the basis of their assessment. In truth, we cannot control how people see things or how, ultimately, they choose to interpret events. What we can control is our attitude when seeking to honour the Lord and serve others. If our eyes are on Him and our motives are pure, and we are doing all we can to be sensitive to the context of our world at that moment, then we must let it fall where it falls. However, let us never confuse audacity with arrogance. The former, as we have seen, can be empty of self yet bold and courageous, whereas the latter is always full of self and tends to leave a bad smell rather than a fragrant perfume in the room! The Lord has little patience with arrogance, in fact He resists any attempt at self-inflation in His presence, but He loves humility, however it is dressed, and He welcomes such an attitude to a higher place.

Her service was Kind
The layout of the room needs to be understood if we are to make sense of the actions of the woman and their impact specifically on Simon. The text informs us that Jesus was "reclining" and this is a clue that the room was set out differently from a typical 21st Century Western home. The likelihood is that the table on which the food was placed would have been U-shaped, just a few feet high, with couches or cushions positioned around the U. The host would take his place at the top left hand side of the U as we look at it, and the probability is that Jesus, the "chief guest" would have been sitting directly opposite at the top right hand side of the U. Those reclining would generally lean on their left arm and reach over and eat with their right hand. Thus Simon and Jesus would be facing one another, with the other guests positioned around the table. When we get this, it makes total sense of much of the detail in the rest of the story – namely, where the woman stood (behind the feet of Jesus), how she ministered to Jesus' feet (she's not under the table, she at the end of His couch in full public view), the fact that Simon could see everything (he had a direct view across the table) and the dramatic moment when Jesus turns to the woman and

speaks to Simon (we'll get to that later in the book). Though seeking to be as sensitive as possible, the woman was in full public view.

Look at what Dr Luke tells us:

"She began to wet His feet with her tears..." (v38)

As we read the story chronologically, we're not aware at this point that Jesus' feet have not been cleaned. It's later that Jesus points this out to His host, as the actions of the woman are held up in contrast. As we've observed already, this was a basic social etiquette extended to any guest and, of course, it also made good hygiene sense. After all, who wants to recline next to the guy with the smelly feet? The wealthy of Jesus' world would have assigned servants to wash the feet of their guests as they entered, removing the sand, grime, sweat and whatever else may have attached itself. Their sandals or shoes were left outside and guests would enter barefoot into the home and hospitality area, enabling them to recline feeling comfortable and refreshed.

In a dramatic event with His own disciples, no servant was around to wash feet and apparently none of Jesus' young followers were prepared to step up and do it, so Jesus Himself took the place of a servant and stooped to wash the feet of His friends and followers. This was a truly shocking moment that they would never forget, and which John, the beloved and youngest disciple in the group, records in precise detail.[7]

There are two things to note as the woman starts to minister to Jesus' feet.

Firstly, in order to do so, she had to kneel down and reduce herself to a physically low position. If her tears are to do their work, if her hair is to take the role of a towel and if her lips are to touch His flesh, then she could not remain standing behind

Him; those actions required her to kneel as low as possible to reach the feet of Jesus.

Secondly, His feet were still dirty! Imagine the look of sandaled feet after a day of walking. Think of the sweat and dirt mingled together. Consider the smell and remember that the feet were not simply the lowest part of the body, but were regarded as low. In the days of Jesus if you wanted to insult someone's town, you would knock the dust "off your feet", symbolising *their* dust wasn't worthy of *your* feet.[8] Bad practice would be to lift your foot to someone, or worse still, hit them with your sandal or shoe. Though these were the feet of Jesus, they were still filthy and lowly!

With no water offered to her she "wet His feet with her tears". The use of the word **bréchō** implies the strength and volume of her tears. The woman was not just having a little weep but, as one commentator suggested, her tears fell like a shower of rain. So strong were her tears that she was able to wash away the grime on His feet and do for Him what His host had not offered.

Though it is a little more romantic to see her tears as an act of worship, we must not rush past the fact that this was also literally an act of service and kindness. His feet had not been washed, so she washed them for Him, allowing her worship of Him and service for Him to mingle into a single act. Her service expressed her worship and her worship was her service. Without words … much was said!

Paul encouraged believers to "…offer your bodies as a living sacrifice…" in an act of true worship unto God.[9] Later he would remind the Corinthians as they struggled with issues of corporate and life-worship:

"You are not your own; you were bought at a price. Therefore honour God with your bodies."[10]

While of his own life Paul emphatically declared, "For me to live is Christ!"[11]

In the 21st Century Church we must be careful not to reduce worship to something a band delivers on a Sunday morning, or to singing a few songs off an electronic screen in our gatherings. As much as I love the explosion of great songs and worship genres, we must not succumb to the false dichotomy of allowing our lifestyle to be divorced from our worship. It's not an either/or scenario, but rather both/and. Worship is confession and conduct. Worship is words and works. Worship is song and service. In fact, I would push a little further and suggest that truly extravagant worship happens when our confession is expressed through our conduct, when our words are heard in our works, and when our songs boom out in our service. If the only time we worship is when we're in a building with a bunch of other worshippers, audacity is less of a requirement. It's in the real world that our worship needs to be heard, in the public, hostile and unsuspecting places, where many have not encountered the Lord or the extravagance of His followers. Imagine if our worship for Him didn't just happen where *we* are, but it happened where *they* are!

I'm not appealing for worship bands on the streets (though that would be a good thing too), but rather worshippers in their world. Yes, let's lift our hands and voices in our gatherings, but let's also get our hands dirty in our world. Let's serve our local church, but let's also serve our broken world. Let's make sure that worship isn't just a private affair, but a matter of public record.

The extravagance of the woman is released through relatively simple things. She was *intentional* – she made a decision to do the right thing wherever He was and whatever it cost. She was *audacious* – her aim was not to offend but to offer her love and gratitude to Jesus. She was not responsible for how others read it, only how she did it. She was *kind* – though the alabaster jar would be eventually broken, her Saviour's feet were dirty and someone needed to clean them ... so why not her? Her service became her worship and her worship was expressed in her service. Without songs, or support, or atmosphere, her extravagance was clear for all to see and hear.

If today we followed the lead of this woman, imagine what might happen. Think of the impact on our world if we all went out and decided to be **Intentional, Audacious** and **Kind,** creating a context where extravagance was normal not occasional. I pray our songs will be heard in our service!

Endnotes
1. Genesis 1:1
2. John 1:14
3. John 3:16
4. Galatians 4:4
5. Ephesians 1:4
6. See Psalms 136
7. John 13
8. Matthew 10:14
9. Romans 12:1
10. 1 Corinthians 6:19-20
11. Philippians 1:21

Chapter 3 – Tools of the Trade
Extravagant Statement

As the shock-filled silence enveloped the room, the only sound heard was that of the woman raining tears onto the feet of Jesus. Host and guests alike seemed paralysed by the spectacle, knowing that something should be done, but not quite knowing what. Jesus is still reclining with His back to her, while Simon is transfixed, and his guests are reduced to helpless spectators. In the hesitancy created by her *extravagant service* the woman does what any servant would do to feet that have just been washed, she proceeds to dry them. However, instead of reaching for a towel, the text tells us,

"...then she wiped them with her hair..." (v38)

Her hair was used as a towel to "wipe His feet dry". The word translated "wipe" is **ekmássō,** meaning *from to handle or wipe,* hence to wipe off or wipe dry. In fact, it's the same word used of Jesus in John 13, when He stooped to serve His friends by washing their feet.

"After that, He poured water into a basin and began to wash His disciples' feet, ***drying them*** with the towel that was wrapped around Him." (John 13:5)

Just as Jesus dried the feet of His followers with His towel, so the woman uses her hair in the same way to dry off the feet of Jesus. This was therefore not a casual action, requiring a gentle swish of her hair. Rather, to dry His feet properly it would have taken both effort and time as every part of the foot (even between the toes) were wiped clean.

Some might ask, so what? What's the big deal if she used her hair or a towel? In order for the woman's hair to be used in this way, it had to be unbound, so as to hang long and loose. Though the text is not explicit, the woman either entered Simon's house with her hair covered or possibly bound up. If a woman in the world of Jesus displayed loose hair in public, this would have been regarded, at best, as immodesty and at worst, immorality. In fact, some religious groups would permit a husband the right to divorce his wife if she displayed her hair publicly in such a provocative way. One scholar, Joel Green, describes her behaviour as "erotic" and therefore "outrageous", concluding that letting hair down "would have been on a par with appearing topless in public."[1]

Of course, Green is not suggesting that the woman was being erotic, but certainly her actions might have been interpreted as such. Though it is likely that the woman initially abided by the social convention of the day by covering her hair (with uncovered hair she would have been spotted long before reaching Jesus), it is clear that in this action of unrestrained devotion she uncovers and possibly unbinds her hair, using it to dry Jesus' feet. At first glance, this action might be seen simply as one of practical necessity. After all, His feet are wet and she needs a towel. With nothing close to hand, she uses her hair. But a closer look suggests that the use of the woman's hair points to something much more significant – that in fact her hair carries a weighty symbolism which becomes the vehicle of a profoundly *extravagant statement*. Her hair is not merely a towel but a testimony, and through its use she speaks to Jesus, and anyone else in the room that has ears to hear.

So what can we hear through this *extravagant statement*?

She was letting go of her old past

Some have suggested that this woman was a prostitute, even though there is nothing explicit in the text to substantiate this. The woman is referred to as a sinner twice in the passage, once by Doctor Luke, "...who lived a sinful life..." (v37) and once by Simon, "...and what kind of a woman she is – that she is a sinner" (v39). The same word is used in both instances and it points to the idea of "missing the mark or deviating from the path". It is clear that Simon knew who the woman was and by implication so did his guests. Her reputation had preceded her and once she uncovered, everyone knew who she was. It's this sense of being "well known" in her town that moves some to suggest she was a prostitute, or at the very least, a woman generous with sexual favours.

We should not become distracted by an argument around whether the woman was a prostitute or not, but neither should we rush past the message that her uncovered hair might be communicating to Jesus and the room. If she was into the sin implied in the text, then her hair would have been a valuable tool of her trade and men would pay for her hair to be unbound for them. In exchange for money or gifts, this woman's hair may have pleasured men of her town and maybe even men in that room. Some have suggested that the actions of this woman are not unlike those of slave girls, who in the more liberal, hedonistic contexts of the Greco-Roman world, would fondle the feet of dinner party guests as a precursor to sexual favours.

If she was who we think she was, then the unsolicited use of her "expensive" hair as a towel on the feet of Jesus is one of the most extravagant statements she can make to Him. In letting down her hair she is in fact letting go of her past, making a public declaration of allegiance to Jesus, and literally laying down the "tools of her trade" at His feet. No longer would her hair be uncovered for money, and no longer would it be used for the trade of sin. Now, in this gloriously extravagant moment, her hair, her past, the person she was, is surrendered to Jesus.

We all have a past. For some it is, relatively speaking, pain-free and ordinary, yet for others the past represents trauma, brokenness and a lifestyle that was far from God's best for our lives. Yet, no matter who you are or what your past looks like, we all, without exception, have to place our past at the feet of Jesus and allow Him to transform our view of it. Our past will go with us wherever we go, but it does not have to control or define us. It is interesting that Simon refers to the woman as a sinner in the present tense – "she is a sinner" – when it was clear that's what she *was*. People may see us through what has been, but the Lord sees us through what He has done. If we have the courage to lay it down, He has the power to transform our view of it, ensuring we are people with a past, without living in that past or letting it live in us.

In the same Gospel, Jesus tells a story of a father with two lost sons, usually referred to as the parable of the prodigal son. The story is found in Luke 15 and, as we've already seen, the context is important. Sinners surrounded Jesus, with the religious on the fringes of the party. In response to their criticism He tells the story of a son (the youngest) who asked for his inheritance early and left home for a far off country. Things didn't work out and the young man now returns to the father in the hope that at least he will be accepted as a servant. However, the response of the father is remarkable, and demonstrates for us his attitude to both his son and his past, through four transformational actions.

Firstly, he rescued what was condemned

"But while he was still a long way off, his father saw him and was filled with compassion for him; he ran to his son, threw his arms around him and kissed him." (Luke 15:20)

It's easy to see this as a concerned father, watching for his son and running to greet him … but there is something deeper and more sinister at work here. The father is not running to greet his son, *but to save him.*

In the world of Jesus, if a young man lost his inheritance to the gentiles, the village would break a large pot in front of him and cry, "[Name] is cut off from the people." The community would then have nothing to do with him. This was known as *Kezazah* – "the cutting off". Hence the father runs (something men of his standing would never do) to save his son from the condemnation that awaited him.[2]

Secondly, he redeemed what was lost

Note, the father does not respond to the lament of his son in verse 21, instead he gives an order:

"Quick! Bring the best robe and put it on him." (v22)

He wasn't ordering the son's best robe, but the best robe in the house, and as Bailey so beautifully points out, the best robe would be the father's robe.[3]

The son was not given one of his own robes, but the *best* robe his father owned. I love the idea of redemption within the

New Testament. It doesn't simply point to being bought *from* something, but it also points to being bought *to* something. We are redeemed (or bought) *from, to live for!* In this action the son is redeemed from his past and brought to a new place as a son.

Thirdly, he renewed what was broken

"Put a ring on his finger..." (v22)

The ring in question would have most likely been the signet ring of the family, carrying the family mark and authority. By placing the ring on his son's finger, the father was renewing a broken relationship that would have shamed his whole household and broken his heart. As Bailey points out, "the problem is not the broken law, but the broken relationship"[4] and this can only be fixed by an action of immense generosity.

Fourthly, he Restored what was stolen

"...and sandals on his feet." (v22)

In a world where slaves went barefoot and sons wore shoes,[5] this action would have been powerful for the listening audience. A foolish decision and reckless living had stolen the life and wealth of the father's son for a little while. He had reached rock-bottom by serving the pigs and no doubt still smelt of pig when he returned home. But now that he had returned, all that was gone. The father was determined that his son would not enter his home barefoot like a slave (that's what the son expected), but he would enter it with sandals on his feet ... because that's what sons do.

I love how Bailey concludes around this moment:

"The son now faces the temptation to indulge in false humility ... He overcomes this last temptation and in genuine humility accepts restoration, knowing that he is totally unworthy. Everything he has is due to his father's love and bounty."[6]

Like the son, this woman had been confronted by the compassion of Jesus, who refused to condemn her, but instead rescued, redeemed, renewed and restored her. By the time she reached the feet of Jesus that night, her past had already been dealt with, and therefore this became a moment of celebration and identification with what Jesus had done. By using her hair as a towel, she resisted the temptation of false humility, but instead, in genuine humility embraced and accepted His grace, understanding that everything she now had was due to His love and bounty!

Extravagance is not birthed in brilliance, but brokenness; in the recognition that it is only by His grace that we are free. In all our growing let us never forget that He rescued, redeemed, restored and renewed our lives. If we keep that in mind, extravagance will never be far from our hearts!

She was embracing a new purpose
As she toweled His feet with her hair, she was not only letting go of her past, but I believe she was embracing her new purpose and the opportunity that now lay before her as a follower of Jesus. It's interesting that immediately after this story, Luke tells us that as Jesus travelled around, not only were the twelve with Him, but...

"...also some women who had been cured of evil spirits and diseases: Mary (called Magdalene) from whom seven demons had come out; Joanna wife of Chuza, the manager of Herod's household; Susanna; and many others. These women were helping to support them out of their own means." (Luke 8:2-3)

We can't be certain that this woman was among those women, but it is a striking coincidence that immediately after Jesus' anointing, we are given insight into the women who followed and supported Him – the clear implication being that they too were His disciples.

In the world before Jesus met her, this woman was self-centred doing only what she wanted. She pleasured men for money and lived life as she wanted to live it. But now things have changed. She's not accepting wealth, she's giving it. She's not doing things because someone has asked her, rather she's lavishly serving Jesus because it's what she wants to do. Whereas *she* was the centre of her world, now *He* has become the centre and with that reality, everything has changed. What looks like the inappropriate behaviour of a sinful woman is actually a "monument of sacred affection".[7]

A similar offer is given to another unnamed woman, caught in the act of adultery, as recorded in John 8:1-11. Although there is controversy around the inclusion of this story in the Canon of Scripture, for me the spirit of it fits perfectly with the person and message of Jesus. In the story it is clear that the woman is guilty and deserves to die, yet by the end, every accuser has gone and only Jesus is left with her. His words drip of grace and truth, echoing both the unmerited favour expressed in unconditional love and the offer of forgiveness, along with the challenge to leave behind her life of self-centred destruction and to embrace the opportunity to live a new way.

"Then neither do I condemn you … Go now and leave your life of sin." (v11)

Leaving our past is one thing, but grabbing a new future, a God-given purpose is something else, and the former does not necessarily lead to the latter. It is not enough to leave what has been, but Jesus calls us to live in what He has for us now and in the future. Having let go of her past, the woman is now grabbing hold of her new purpose, and all of this is captivated in the hair toweling of His feet. The woman has been given a second chance at a life of hope and purpose and she grabs it with both hands!

One of my best friends in the whole world is a man called Alan Graham. We went to Bible College together in 1984 and a friendship was forged that has lasted ever since. On 3rd June 1980, Alan Graham's life was radically changed. At 28 years old, his marriage was about to disintegrate and his life was a mess. He stumbled out of a pub and into an outreach event that a local church was holding. That night, in a drunken stupor, he surrendered his life to Jesus. Though skeptical at first, his wife Dorothy also became a follower of Jesus and within six months they were heavily involved in sharing Jesus with as many people as they could find and with anyone who would listen. Their hearts were drawn to children and soon they were running Good News Clubs for children all over Belfast.

God eventually took them to Donegal, Ireland, where, in the space of twelve years, they established an amazing network of children's clubs and camps reaching approximately 1,600 children a month. I remember visiting his work in the North West of Ireland, covering hundreds of miles to take school assemblies and clubs. Alan seemed to know the name of every child and he remembered minute details, such as the fact that one boy's cat had just had kittens. As we crossed a playground in one school, a little boy, new to that particular school, approached myself and Alan. He said something I will never forget till the day I die: "Mr Graham, are you the 'Good News' man?"

Now, Alan and Dorothy are in Zimbabwe ministering

tirelessly to street children, orphans, A.I.D.S. victims, schools and clubs. Through their generosity hundreds are fed, clothed and given the chance of an education. They run perhaps one of the best children's homes in the whole of Zimbabwe, an oasis of heaven on earth called Jabulani, and on a daily basis they lavishly give themselves away to those they meet, resulting in thousands of children being powerfully impacted by the Good News. In 1999 they went out to Zimbabwe with nothing established, but today as I write, they minister to over 20,000 children a month.

Alan didn't just accept God's grace that night through the offer of forgiveness and freedom from alcohol, but he realised that having "freely received" he should "freely give"; having been set free, he should now take hold; having been given a second chance by Jesus, it was his responsibility to make the most of it.

Letting go is good, but taking hold is better! Accepting His forgiveness is life changing, but surrendering to His purpose is world changing.

She was expressing a changed philosophy

How did the woman know what to do? Why did the woman do what she did?

No one coached her, asked her or showed her … yet that night she did something which, 2000 years later, still stands out as an incredible act of extravagance. Her actions are on one level sensuous and, some might suggest, erotic, and though to the pure all things are pure, it is easy to misunderstand the motives of a woman who behaves in such a way. Clearly she is touching Him, through her tears, her long hair, her relentless kisses and her expensive perfume (we'll observe the latter two in the next few chapters). In another context, with another man at another time, these actions may have in fact been erotic, sexual and saturated with sensuality. But in this context with this man on this night, what looks impure is pure, what seems inappropriately intimate is actually true worship, and what may be mistaken as sexual is deeply spiritual. Dare I say, the actions of this woman and a prostitute may possibly look similar, but what transformed the questionable into something glorious was the heart attitude and motivation at the centre of it.

In her previous life, this woman may have done this for money, but in this new life, she's doing it for love. Her uncovered hair once used for sin, is now used for service – though to the untrained eye, to the heart not tuned to the Spirit of God, it looks like the same thing.

Have you ever wondered why Jesus doesn't react? Until He speaks to Simon, Jesus seems to be carrying on as if nothing out of the ordinary is happening, perhaps enjoying the olives laid on by His host – and all the while the woman is doing what she's doing. Perhaps He doesn't react to her for the same reason that He reacts to Simon – because He knew the heart of both her actions and of his words!

From the beginning of the Scriptures we observe that the belief which motivates any action is as important (if not more important) to the Lord than the action itself. In fact, the Lord would rather have obedience that is true than sacrifice that is false, for He doesn't just judge the surface, but sees the spirit. A generous heart can elevate one offering over the other. A sincere heart can form a prayer that changes a nation. A humble heart can see a king in a shepherd boy and an obedient heart can give all out of nothing.

Paul reminds us that it is by the "renewing of our mind" that our behaviour is transformed and that the source of our mind's renewal is by receiving sight or revelation of God's truth by His Spirit.[8] Without revelation we are left with information only, which, at best, produces behavioural modification but not lasting transformation. The danger is that information makes us clever, whereas revelation can make us better. Information has the power to merely inform, whereas revelation has the power to transform.

When praying for the church at Ephesus, Paul said,

"I keep asking that the God of our Lord Jesus Christ, the glorious Father, may give you the spirit of wisdom and revelation, so that you may know Him better. I pray also that the eyes of your heart may be enlightened in order that you may know the hope to which He has called you, the riches of His glorious inheritance in the saints, and His incomparably great power for us who believe." (Ephesians 1:17-19)

Note the repeated emphasis from Paul on seeing something and knowing something, that by implication brings transformation. For Paul there seems to be a pattern of, *seeing – knowing – doing.*

"… the spirit of wisdom and revelation, so that you may know Him better." (v17)

The word translated *revelation* here is **apokálupsis** meaning "from to reveal" or "to uncover, to unveil and to reveal". Paul argues that something we can't learn by mere human effort or logic needs to be revealed to us, so we can supernaturally change in form.

The word translated *know* (Him) in this phrase is **epígnōsis** meaning to recognise. It expresses a more thorough participation in the acquiring of knowledge in the learner. In other words, the learner has come to know by engaging with the process at hand; they have come to learn something they did not know before.

Another way of phrasing this line might be, "I pray God uncovers something to you so you can recognise and participate in Him."

Note the second part of the emphasis:

"...the eyes of your heart may be enlightened so that you may know the hope to which He has called you..." (v18)

The word translated *enlightened* is **phōtízō** meaning "to give light to something, to shine a light upon". We might think of walking into a dark room where our eyes can't quite make out what is in front of us, but the minute we turn the light on we can see everything before us. Paul is asking that God's torch will shine into our hearts so we can see clearly what may have eluded us before.

The word translated to *know* (hope) is **oída** meaning "to know intuitively or instinctively". Note, it's a different word than before. Paul seems to be suggesting that when God's light shines into our hearts we can come to know spiritual things intuitively; they come to us without having known such things beforehand.

Is this what we see in the actions of the woman that night in Simon's house? Has she come to know because something has been revealed? Is her uncovered hair a sign of her unveiled eyes? Are her actions flowing out of an intuitive understanding of what the Lord wants without having been told or taught? Does she know instinctively that it's the right thing to do because a divine torch has been shone into her heart?

It is revelation of Him that transforms her actions from

superficially sensuous to deeply spiritual. It is an enlightened heart that showed her what to do that night resulting in pure worship that touched much more than the feet of Jesus. Her uncovered hair is not the work of a prostitute, but the product of a new philosophy, a new way of thinking; eyes that have been opened and a heart that now has God's light shining within it.

When the woman uncovered her hair that night and let it hang long and loose, she made an *extravagant statement* to Jesus, the sound of which was not lost on Him. As her hair caressed His feet, toweling them dry, she was letting everyone in the room know that her world had changed forever. As she swept the dirt from His feet, so too her past was gone, swept away by His grace. As she took hold of her hair, ensuring she did a thorough job of drying His feet, so she was taking hold of a new day, a second chance being afforded to her by His unconditional love. As she ministered to His feet, not because she was paid or asked to do so, but as a result of a revelation of truth, her actions were redeemed, transformed and elevated to an act of spiritual worship.

Endnotes

1. Green, J., *The Gospel of Luke*, Eerdmans, 1997, pp.309-310
2. Bailey, K.E., *The Cross and the Prodigal*, IVP Books, 2005, p.52
3. Bailey, p.71
4. Bailey, p.59
5. Bailey, p.71
6. Bailey, p.72
7. Danker, F.W., *Commentary on Luke: Jesus and the New Age*, Fortress, 1988, pp.169-170
8. Romans 12:1-2

Chapter 4 – No Subtitles Required
Extravagant Surrender

With the prospect of Jesus' feet being *thoroughly* dried by the woman's uncovered hair, Simon and his guests might have expected some respite from the outrageous spectacle, but it was simply the signal for a whole new level of discomfort! No sooner were the feet of Jesus dry, than the woman began to kiss them: "...then she wiped them with her hair, kissed them..." The word used here is **kataphileō** and can simply mean to kiss, but interestingly, every time Dr Luke uses it, it points to kissing that is eager, passionate or repetitive.

Aside from this story, Luke uses it on two other occasions. We have seen one reference already, in the story of the *Lost Sons*, when Jesus says of the father,

"...he ran to his son, threw his arms around him and **kissed him**." (Luke 15:20)

We see it again when Paul is about to leave the leaders of the church at Ephesus,

"They all wept as they embraced him and **kissed him**." (Acts 20:37)

When reading our story, it's easy to get the impression that the woman kissed the feet of Jesus once and moved on to the anointing part. But the construction of the word (identical to Acts 20), points to an action that is not only intentional and passionate, but continuous: "then she continued kissing His feet…"[1] When we put the three references together in Luke's writings, it seems she kissed His feet just like the father kissed his son and the elders kissed Paul. This was a moment of *extravagant surrender*. In Luke 7, some might suggest that the kissing element of this story is a typically *feminine action*, placing it in a stereotypical box. But when we look at the other examples afforded to us, it's probable that it's almost entirely men that are doing the kissing, allowing us to view our story, not so much as the actions of a woman, but of a worshipper!

Within our story, there is a contrast between the kiss (or lack of) of Simon and the kiss of the woman. When Jesus confronts Simon as recorded in verse 45 He says,

"You did not give me a kiss, but this woman, from the time I entered, has not stopped kissing my feet."

When referring to Simon's *non-kiss*, Jesus used the word **phílēma**, used generally in the context of a kiss of greeting or a kiss as a sign of friendship and love (and interestingly the same word that Jesus used when describing how Judas kissed Him in the act of betrayal).[2] This, however, is contrasted to **kataphileō** used by both Jesus (7:45) and Luke (7:38) to describe the woman's actions. Her kiss was a passionate kiss. It's through the lens of this contrast that I want us to view the woman's kisses, to see what her extravagant surrender might teach us.

Greeting and Gratitude
When greeting friends, family and guests, kissing the face and/ or the hands would have been expected and accepted in the 1st Century world of Jesus, and in fact within early Christianity. No doubt influenced by this Jewish custom, the kiss developed

into a symbol of spiritual kinship and community. It would have been surprising and noticeable for Simon the host not to greet Jesus, his chief guest, in this way – an issue that Jesus explicitly references: "...you did not give Me a kiss...". Jesus expected Simon to kiss Him but, for whatever reason, it did not happen.

The lack of greeting is in contrast to the relentless kisses of the woman as she expressed her gratitude to Jesus for "cancelling her debt". Jesus suggests that she had not stopped kissing His feet, highlighting the fact that Simon did not offer just one kiss while she offered a multitude. Furthermore, though Simon struggled to kiss the face of his guest, she had no problem lavishing her love onto His feet.

Why the contrast?

I suspect it was an issue of *focus*. Simon may been preoccupied by who else was in the room that night, conscious that his actions would be noted and scrutinised by those opposed to Jesus. Though Jesus was his guest, Simon was very much playing to the gallery, and it was crucial that he preformed well. The greeting snub was probably intentional and would have been designed to score points with his guests, while making a point to Jesus. Don't get me wrong, Simon saw Jesus and knew exactly what was going on, but the tragedy is, he *really* didn't see Jesus. Though Jesus was there in front of him, in reality, other issues and people were preoccupying his focus.

The woman had no such dilemma. In fact, for her, it's the very opposite. I suspect she was so focused on Jesus that she could not see anyone else. Yes, she knew it was Simon's house and, before doing what she did, she would have noticed the

VIPs in the room – but as her eyes fixed on Jesus, they became peripheral figures to the main event. As we watch the woman, we are impressed by her focus and by the fact that nothing seems to be distracting her from what she wants to do. Her gallery has *One occupant*, and at that moment, He is all that matters to her!

The writer to the Hebrews encourages us to,

"…fix our eyes on Jesus…" (Hebrews 12:2)

The word translated fix is **aphoráō** meaning "to look away", pointing to the idea of looking away steadfastly or intently towards something or someone. The writer wants us to be aware of the great "cloud of witnesses" (v1), but doesn't want them to preoccupy our vision. Instead, when it comes to focus, they are on the periphery and Jesus is at the centre, for that is the only way we are going to run and finish the race.

This in essence is the idea contained in the 1st Word or Command of God in Exodus and the heart of the *Shema* in Deuteronomy.

In Exodus 20:3 we are told,

"You shall have no other gods before Me."

The Hebrew word translated "before" is פָּנַי (pa-nai) and carries the concept of "before the face". I love the idea that to have no other gods before the Lord is to place nothing between His face and ours; that He is the only One we focus on and see.

In Deuteronomy 6:4 the *Shema* begins,

"Hear O Israel: The Lord our God the Lord is One."[3]

The word translated "one" is **echad**, which doesn't simply carry with it the idea of one, but in this context, the nuance of only, or *alone* – that there is no one like Him. When read like this it makes much more sense and points to the truth that the Lord is alone, therefore we should love Him with all our being. When we know He is alone and when we have Him at the centre of our focus with nothing between our face and His, then the idea of loving Him with all our being becomes a natural and possible expression.

In the light of His aloneness the text says, "…and you shall love the Lord your God with all your heart…". The word translated "heart" is בְּבָל (levav) and can literally point to "the middle" or "the centre", but in this context it clearly points to the "inner person" and thus, the Lord is calling His people to love Him from the centre of their being.

Loving God then is about placing Him deliberately at the centre of our world. We ensure that no other gods are between His face and ours and our focus is consumed by Him and fixed on Him. This is what is happening when the woman relentlessly kisses Jesus' feet. Her eyes are fixed on Him. Nothing is getting between His face and hers. Now that He is at the centre, the only outcome is love, expressed in kisses for Him. He has become her focus, resulting in her extravagant surrender.

If, like Simon, Jesus remains on the periphery and our focus is on others things, then extravagance will evade us and our kisses of worship will never be offered. If however, we understand that He is alone and we have the courage to place Him at the centre, with no thing or person between His face and ours, then we will not be able to stop ourselves from kissing Him with relentless passion, through a lifestyle of worship.

Suspicion and Surrender

Whatever Simon thought or hoped Jesus was, it is clear from his behavoiur that he was uncertain of how to treat the young Rabbi. Normal basic etiquette was not offered to Jesus, namely, water to wash the feet, a kiss of greeting and some scented oil for the evening, all things that Jesus alludes to when confronting His host later in the evening, "... you did not..." (three times). Simon's suspicion of Jesus "... if this man were a prophet..." dictates behaviour of curious caution and almost forensic examination. There is no doubt that whatever is on the menu that night, Simon is hoping that Jesus is one of the courses, and that by the end of the evening he and his friends have either saved the wayward teacher or discredited Him. Simon's suspicion kept Jesus at arms length and therefore far from his heart.

The woman, on the other hand, has no such difficulty. The teaching, compassion and power of Jesus had already entered her heart, as her lips on His feet demonstrated. She *knows* who He is and in kissing His feet gives the strongest signal possible of subservience and devotion. While Simon's suspicions cause him to hesitate around Jesus, her acceptance of Him paved the way for kisses of *extravagant surrender*!

Why the contrast?

I suspect it was an issue of *freedom*. Simon was bound by a well-worked, solid, undeniable logic. He, after all, was a good man, righteous and holy and he represented a community that passionately believed in the Scriptures and would do anything to defend them. What he had been taught clashed with the claims and practices of the Galilean Rabbi and, as any serious person would do, Simon defended what he knew! Jesus sat beyond the world of Simon's understanding, and when faced with such a prospect, one either hardens to the unknown, or in humility explores the world beyond the boundary line. Simon understandably, chose to stand his ground and defend his territory.

To kiss the feet of another so publicly, passionately and continuously suggests the woman had long since crossed the boundary line. Whatever happened to her was so dynamic and life changing that she risked what little reputation she had left in behaviour that could have landed her in serious trouble. But at this moment none of that matters; she is clearly consumed with Jesus, oblivious to the controversy stirring around her, and determined to finish what she started for Him. The freedom she experienced is now expressed in the extravagance of her actions and, having freely received from Jesus, she freely gave.

If we return to the *Shema* for a moment, we are reminded that we are to love the Lord on the basis that He is Lord God alone, and that we are to love Him with all our heart, but also "…with all your soul…". The word "soul" is נֶפֶשׁ (nephesh) and can be understood simply as "soul", but really the idea at the heart of the word is "life". We see this powerfully demonstrated in Genesis 2:7 when it says,

"The Lord God formed the man from the dust of the ground and breathed into his nostrils the breath of life, and the man became a living being."

The human form, clearly that of a man, lay on the ground, perfect in every way, but the body on the ground lacked life, so the Lord breathed life into the body and *it* became *him!* The essence of *nephesh* is the life of God within us that gives us life. The very reason for our existence is because He breathed into us, therefore the greatest act of worship any human can engage in is to return our *nephesh* to God. Having received life from Him, we now surrender that life back to Him.

As human beings we tend to think of life as ours, but the paradigm of Genesis teaches us that life, our life, is His. He is the originator and the giver of that life and His desire is that we understand where our *nephesh* came from and generously return it to Him.

Isn't that what the writer to the Hebrews further hints at? Having told us to "fix our eyes on Jesus", he tells us why:

"… the author and perfector of our faith…" (Hebrews 12:2)

The word "author" is translated from **archēgós**, itself from **arché** meaning "beginning or rule", and **ágō** meaning "to lead". As far as our faith-life is concerned, Jesus is the beginner, the originator, the One who first breathed the *nephesh* of faith into us. Thus, having received faith from Him, we offer the highest from of worship by returning it to Him.

This is what we see in the woman. Her behaviour may not be in line with social etiquette, synagogue rules or Pharisaic practice, but having received into her broken world the breath of God, she gladly and generously surrenders it back to the *Author* by kissing His feet. Simon, it seems, has received logic but not life. He cannot compute the actions of the woman let alone emulate them. Simon is trapped in the small, claustrophobic world of suspicion, while the woman runs free in the wide-open expanse of surrender!

Duty and Desire

Though Simon's lack of social etiquette was bad form, in truth he didn't do anything wrong. There were no laws that said water had to be offered, or a kiss should be extended, or that perfumed oil should be given. These practices and others like them had become part of the pervading culture, but they weren't written in stone as law. These things were good things to do, but they weren't required actions. Therefore, technically, Simon was on safe, moral ground. He had simply chosen not to do these things and no one could therefore criticise him for his choices. For Simon it was enough that Jesus was in his house, which in his context was a very generous gesture. He had fulfilled his duty in opening his home and was under no obligation to go any further. Simon did what he had to!

Though the woman's lack of social etiquette was bad form, in truth, she didn't do anything wrong either. There were no laws within the Torah forbidding the specific actions of the woman. In fact, to kiss the feet of a Rabbi was, in her day, a sign of deep respect and acceptance. Her behaviour may have been questionable, but it wasn't immoral or illegal. It should be noted too that her behaviour wasn't required. Jesus, throughout His ministry, transformed many lives but there were no prescriptive requirements on "how to respond once one's life has been changed". Jesus didn't ask for this from the woman, but she gave it nonetheless. It would have been enough for the woman to follow Jesus – she didn't have to turn up that night and do what she did. But what everyone witnessed from her was not duty, but desire. She wanted to wash His feet! She wanted to kiss them! She wanted to pour the most expensive possession she owned on Him. Simon was trapped by duty but the woman was liberated by desire! Simon did what he had to and no more. She did what she wanted and gave all she had!

Why the contrast?

I suspect it was an issue of *fervour*.

Our English word fervour finds its origin in the Latin word *fervere*, which means "to boil". As the kettle or saucepan comes to the boil, it is coming to a place of fervour. It is not cold or lukewarm; rather fervour is synonymous with hotness, energy, passion and intensity. As water is brought to the boil by heat, so passion, enthusiasm and intensity have a heat source; something within that is pushing it to boiling point!

If we return to the *Shema* once again, this lies at the heart of the third expression of love. Not only are we told "and you shall love" the Lord with all your heart and life, but we are to love him "…with all your strength". The word is מְאֹד (me'od) and literally translates as "very" or "muchness"! This, of course, makes no sense in English, but the idea points to "force, energy and enthusiasm". In other words, *with all you've got*! The connection of the text is clear. If we see the Lord God as "alone", that there is no one like Him, and we understand what He has done for us, then giving Him our fervour, our passion and our *very*, should be the natural outcome. Our *very* usually follows where our vision leads!

This again is echoed by the writer to the Hebrews in the passage we've referred to. Having told us to "fix our eyes" on Jesus because He is the "author and perfector" of our faith, he concludes,

"…who for the joy set before Him endured the cross…"

The phrase "set before Him" is from the word **prókeimai** which itself is made up of two words, *pró* – "before" and *keímai* – "to be laid, set or lie before". Something is set or laid before Jesus and it's that something which is *causing* His joy. His joy is not random, coming from a happy personality type, rather His joy is coming from something He sees, something that now stands before Him. He has a reason for His joy and His fervour has a focus. Something other than the horror of the cross is bringing Him to the boil!

The only time Simon shows some passion that night is in his

reaction to the behaviour of the woman, and even that stays under control inside his head. He is the model of stoicism, a man under control with no threat that anything will come to the boil, especially his appreciation of Jesus.

For the woman, on the other hand, her passion was so strong that it took her all her energy not to act sooner, and when she began, her fervour boiled over in relentless worship-filled enthusiasm. Simon cannot get going because there's no heat within him bringing things to the boil. The woman it seems, cannot stop coming to the boil because the heat within her is so strong. "… she has been forgiven much…".

No doubt Simon could recite the *Shema* off by heart and probably did so every morning and evening, but it was the woman who practised its driving heart that night. Brought to the boil by His love, mercy and grace, she kissed His feet with a relentless tenderness, in the way that one might kiss the face of their lover. For Simon, Jesus was a Rabbi, but for the woman He was a Saviour. For Simon, Jesus is to be examined, but for the woman He is there to be embraced. Simon does what he has to, while she does all she can. Simon refused Jesus a simple kiss of greeting, while she lavished on His feet kisses of gratitude.

Extravagant surrender has less to do with personality and more to do with purpose and passion. The woman's kisses flowed from a heart transformed by the goodness and lovingkindness of the Lord. Having freely received, she freely gave. It is easy to relegate her kisses to gender, culture, context or even personality type – and no doubt these may all play a part – but to do so is to miss the beating heart of this moment. In kissing Him so relentlessly, she is declaring that He is *Lord alone* and with each kiss, she is expressing her love for Him

71

with all her heart, life and strength! It seems that though Simon knew the *Shema*, the woman truly heard it!

Endnotes

1. The New Revised Standard Version

2. Luke 22:48

3. **Shema** carries the idea to hear, but more than that… having heard, we do! It's hearing with action. It has 3 sections found in Dt.6 as above and Dt.11:13-21 & Num.13:37-41. It was normally receipted every morning and evening.

Chapter 5 – All Or Nothing
Extravagant Sacrifice

The final act of the woman's extravagance was heralded by an unmistakeable cracking sound, as her alabaster jar was broken open. When describing the other anointing of Jesus, Mark tells us explicitly, "she broke the jar and poured perfume on His head,"[1] and although as I've established these are two different events, the *alabaster jar* used in both stories forms a common link between the two and, therefore, I assume similar practice. Her perfume was kept to the end, gracing feet that had been washed with tears, dried with hair and lavished with kisses. As the ointment flowed from the open jar, a spectacular and evocative aroma rose and filled the room, as everyone present experienced the power of her liberated fragrance. Her tears were an act of *extravagant service*, while her uncovered hair made an *extravagant statement*. As her kisses were the sign of *extravagant surrender*, so the broken jar and flowing perfume represented a climatic demonstration of *extravagant sacrifice*!

As we watch the woman break open the alabaster jar and apply the contents generously to the feet of Jesus, what do we learn from this moment of extravagance?

Her extravagant sacrifice was expensive

Clues as to the expense of the woman's gift are given in the story.

Firstly, the name alabaster derives from the city of Alabastron in Egypt, which was famous for the manufacture of vases and jars made for the perfume trade.[2] The stone was usually white and translucent, although it was sometimes coloured, and it resembled marble in its appearance, though much softer in texture. If it was designed to contain precious ointment, then the long slim neck was sealed and had to be broken to release its contents.

Secondly, though Luke simply refers to the contents of the jar as perfume, Mark tells us "…a woman came with an alabaster jar of very expensive perfume, made of pure nard."[3] Again, using the two stories as possible comparison, if the alabaster jar in Luke 7 contained something similar to that of Mark 14, then we get an insight into the quality of the contents. Nard was made from a herb, from the *Valerianaceae* family that grows in the Himalayan countries of Bhutan, Nepal and Kashmir in India. The fragrant root and lower stems were dried and used to produce this perfumed ointment. Just a glance at the lengths to which one would have to go in order to obtain such perfume suggests to us it would not be cheap.[4]

Thirdly, when estimating the cost of Mary's offering, Matthew, Mark and John all record that it was worth at least one year's salary (300 denarii), one denarius being the usual daily wage for a labourer in the days of Jesus. John tells us specifically that it was Judas who added the price tag, and as the treasurer (who liked money a little too much), he should know![5]

Fourthly, this type of bottled perfume is only mentioned twice in the whole New Testament. Could it be that the rarity of references to nard perfume in alabaster jars is an affirmation of the expense of such an item – beyond the financial reach of many in Jesus' world?

Everything about this offering screams expensive. Consider your own salary for a moment, or if that doesn't apply, that of someone you love. Imagine taking what you earn annually (pre-tax), putting it all in a jar and giving every single penny of it away to someone else! Now my illustration isn't very scientific and there will be those who want to argue or play with the numbers, but don't go there ... just for a moment, catch the spirit of this idea: giving a gift of the equivalent value of your gross annual salary!

By very definition, extravagance always costs. If we're still happy to go with our definition – *passing the bounds of reason, wild, absurd, flamboyant, abundant or even wasteful* – none of this can be achieved without some dent being made to our reserves, whether they be spiritual, physical, emotional or financial. As we've already seen, these actions were not random or spontaneous and the very fact that the woman arrived at Simon's house with the alabaster jar means that she had already made up her mind to use it – and, we assume, counted the cost of doing so. Extravagance doesn't mean that our offering will be the most expensive item in the room, but it will have demanded considerable cost and significant sacrifice.

The American Crisis is a collection of articles written by Thomas Paine during the American Revolutionary War. In 1776 Paine wrote *Common Sense*, an extremely popular and successful pamphlet arguing for independence from England. The essays collectively constitute Paine's ongoing support for an independent and self-governing America. General Washington found the first essay so inspiring that he ordered that it be read to the troops at Valley Forge. Though no battle took place, Washington's army spent a brutal winter there between 1777 and 1778, costing the lives of almost 3000 soldiers due to malnutrition and sickness.

Paine wrote, "Tyranny, like hell, is not easily conquered; yet we have this consolation with us, that the harder the conflict, the more glorious the triumph. What we obtain too cheap, we esteem too lightly: it is dearness only that gives every thing its value. Heaven knows how to put a proper price upon its goods; and it would be strange indeed if so celestial an article as FREEDOM should not be highly rated."

I love that little sentence tucked away in the paragraph,

"What we obtain too cheap, we esteem too lightly; it is dearness only that gives everything its value."[6]

The value expressed that night in Simon's house was not the price tag on the jar, but rather the estimation the woman had put on Jesus. If it is dearness only that gives everything its value then, to the woman, Jesus was dear indeed. Though I am not suggesting she did not consider the cost (I believe she did), the deciding factor for her was not how precious the alabaster jar was, but how precious He was. He was worth the expense! He was worth the sacrifice! What she now experienced had not been obtained too cheaply and so would not be esteemed too lightly!

What we're prepared to pay says so much about the object of our affections. Too often as observers we can be distracted by the gift, be it a lovely watch, a weekend away, or a necklace. A friend of mine thought it was a good idea to buy his wife a hoover for Christmas. I'll let you decide how that went down! However, the point of a gift is not the gift, but the person you're giving it to. Of course, the gift is important, but it's the means to a greater end. Our giving should never be about drawing attention of *what* we're giving, but rather it throws the spotlight on *who* we're giving it to.

Her extravagant sacrifice was emblematic
In biblical terms, the use of perfume is only mentioned in two contexts.

The first is *worship*, specifically around the work of the Tabernacle and the Temple. In fact, it is here that we see the profession of perfumer appear, not only as something someone did, but as something God wanted.[7] The Lord asked for special perfume to be associated with His presence and the sacred. He was specific about both its ingredients and design.

"Take the following fine spices: 500 shekels of liquid myrrh, half as much (that is, 250 shekels) of fragrant cinnamon, 250 shekels of fragrant calamus, 500 shekels of cassia – all according to the sanctuary shekel – and a hin of olive oil. Make these into a sacred anointing oil, a fragrant blend..." (Exodus 30:22-25)

Metaphorically, the Lord refers to sacrifices made with the right heart in the right way as "...aroma pleasing to the Lord",[8] while offerings made out of disobedient hearts that ignore justice are regarded by Him as a "stench".[9]

The second is *love* and we see this in both a positive and negative context within the Bible.

"While the king was at his table, my perfume spread its fragrance. My beloved is to me a sachet of myrrh resting between my breasts. My beloved is to me a cluster of henna blossoms from the vineyards of En Gedi." (Song of Songs 1:12-14)

"I have covered my bed with coloured linens from Egypt. I have perfumed my bed with myrrh, aloes and cinnamon. Come, let's drink deeply of love till morning; let's enjoy ourselves with love!" (Proverbs 7:16-18)

Both examples sit on the opposite ends of the moral spectrum – the first given in the context of marriage, the second the words of an adulteress or prostitute – but they have one key issue in common. Perfume is used by both to pave the way for something else. In Song of Songs the woman is perfumed and the erotic nature of the image suggests that she is hoping to lead the king from the table to her bed. In Proverbs the bed itself is perfumed with the express intention that they will drink deeply of love on it! The perfume then is not simply about desire, but more significantly about *direction*.

As the ointment touched the feet of Jesus and the perfume filled the air, could it be that the woman's actions were emblematic of both her desire for Him (worship), and the direction she now wished to go, as a lover of Jesus, joined as one in heart? The fact that she is anointing His feet with her perfume is more than coincidental if desire and direction are the essence of what she is saying. His feet benefit from her most expensive possession, as her greatest financial sacrifice is given to the lowliest part of His body, which in itself is only possible if she bows as low as she can go. The perfume is an act of worship by one driven by holy desire and her hope is that it will be an "aroma pleasing to the Lord".

But note too the fact that the perfume is not on her (as in

Song of Solomon) or on her bed (as in Proverbs), but on *His feet*. As we've seen from these texts, perfume was used by both women to point the way to what should happen next, giving as clear a sign as any neon light of their intentions. However, could it be that in anointing His feet with her perfume, she is symbolically sacrificing her own direction and submitting herself to His? By anointing His feet she is saying that she wants to go in His direction, with Him, wherever He leads. Unlike these other women, she does not intend to lead, but follow. Her agenda is not her desire, but rather desire for Him. His feet will lead the way for her life!

Sacrifice that creates the sort of perfume that pleases the Lord is that which contains the ingredients of desire and direction, wholeheartedness and humility, surrender and sacrifice. When He is the object of our desire and we set our course to His direction, I believe we have captured the essence of true worship. If we are not careful, worship can become as much about us (the giver) as the One we're giving it to.

People see what we do, are even attracted by what we do and at times commend us for what we do. Perhaps even that night, people went home and were heard to say, "Did you see what she did?" Whereas the whole point of what she did was so they could *see Him*! Worship, like most things, can become about something it is not and perversely, if we're not careful, worship can be about what *we* feel and what *we* want, when at it's heart, true worship demands that ego and experience be sacrificed to His feet and His will. Though it's impossible not to notice the woman in our story, she tries her hardest not to get in the way of Him. She ministers to His feet, she stays as much on the periphery of the meal table as possible, she gets as low as she can go and she doesn't say a word. All these actions point to the fact that she knows this moment is not about her, but entirely about Him.

"From a human perspective, the act of sacrifice is a process of opening ourselves to God by renouncing something of ourselves. We bring a gift of affection, as a child to a parent. We offer something in our possession, our power, our will, our self-sufficiency. We engage in a symbolic act of renunciation. We acknowledge our dependency on God. Sacrifice is the primal act of love."[10]

True worship is all about the desire with which we come and the direction we are prepared to go. In a world that cries out, "Who am I and why am I here?" the broken alabaster jar calls out, "Who is God and what does He want?" It is interesting that when the Torah speaks about sacrifice, it always connects it to the name Yahweh (the Lord), His more personal yet glorious covenant name, and it never associates sacrifice with Elohim (Elokim), the more impersonal idea of "the force of forces", creator God.[11] The crack of the bottle is the sound of true worship, signifying He is our desire and we will go in His direction.

Her extravagant sacrifice was entire
What made the alabaster jar special and expensive was that it was a one hit offering. It didn't come with a stopper or a pump spray attachment. Once the sealed neck was broken open, the magnificent perfumed ointment inside had to be used. This wasn't a 10% gift or a "see how much I can afford" gift; this offering was all or nothing! The woman had to decide if she wanted to give it or not, knowing she either had to give all

of it, or none of it. By the end of the evening, every ounce of expensive perfume was "wasted" on the feet of the Galilean Rabbi. No other man would ever feel its touch on his skin or experience the wonder of its fragrance. Her Egyptian alabaster jar now lay broken on the floor, while nard made of exotic Asian ingredients soaked into the feet of Jesus. This special possession, saved for the right man and a sacred context, was now gone – the equivalent to a year's salary had vanished into the air.

The book of Leviticus is not one usually associated with passion for most followers of Jesus. In fact, many people I know have never read it, and if they do, they want to get it over with as quickly as possible. However, it is not only part of the Torah (the first five books of the Old Testament or Tanakh), but it is the middle book of the five, forming the "central pillar of its entire edifice."[12] The Hebrew word translated Leviticus is *vayikra* and relates to the opening words of the book,

"The Lord called to Moses…" (Leviticus 1:1)

Vayikra means to call and carries with it the idea of being "summoned in love".

This is further enforced by the second verse of the book,

"When anyone among you *brings* an *offering* to the Lord…" (Leviticus 1:2)

These two words, *brings* and *offering* form the backdrop for the rest of the book, and once understood help us to catch the spirit of Leviticus. The noun translated "offering" is *korban* and points to a gift and/or sacrifice. The verb translated "brings" is *lehakriv*, which at a basic level means to offer something, but also has a deeper nuance implying, "that which is brought close" or the act of "bringing something close". As Rabbi Sacks concludes on this point, "The key element is not so much giving something up (the usual meaning of sacrifice), but rather bringing something close to God."[13]

What a difference it would make to any offering if the focus was not on the cost of the gift, but on the value of the recipient. This is the essence of *vayikra* and why "sacrifice" sits at the heart of everything. The focus was never intended to be on the animal, bird or money, but was always meant to be on the One to whom *korban* was given. The offering was part of the call to come close, because that's what the Lord always wanted: a people who would see Him for Who He was and willingly and generously draw close to Him.

This, of course, was ultimately fulfilled by Jesus Himself, who *drew close* to the Lord by *giving Himself* entirely and unreservedly on the cross, ensuring that humanity in turn could draw close to God through His offering. The Lord gave an offering so that we could draw near to Him and because of this we now have unfettered access to His holy and life-changing presence. Just as in the Tanakh the people of the Lord could draw close to Him because He had first drawn close to them through the call of Abraham, so now, today, we can come near to the Lord with our gifts and offerings, because the Lord has come close to us through Christ Jesus.

Now look again at the woman ... what do you see? At one level it's just a woman giving Jesus some perfume, but at another level, the true level, it is a woman drawing close to the Lord with her gift, because He has drawn close to her and changed her. The expensive gift is willingly and entirely given in a *wild and absurd* way before Simon and his friends, and although misunderstood by all in the room, there is One who grasps exactly what is happening. This so-called sinful woman answered *vayikra* by bringing close her offering, and thus in this moment of abandonment, she captured the spirit of Leviticus and the very heart of Torah!

True extravagant sacrifice as the Lord desires it will never be possible unless we have heard His summons, His love call. Having heard His call and experienced His grace, the gift in our hand is less about cost and loss and more about cause and love. The focus is not on what we're giving, but on Who we are giving it to. We're not consumed with how little we can get away with, but rather we're obsessed with how much we can give. When we hear the call, when His love has truly touched our hearts, it's not about law, what I have to do, but all about love, *what I want to do,* and it's this that transforms our gift from a sacrifice, something we give up, to an offering, something we put in!

One of my favourite hymns is *When I Survey* and the closing verse says:

"Were the whole realm of nature mine,
That were an offering far too small.
Love so amazing, so divine,
Demands my soul, my life, my all."

These words capture the essence of that night in Simon's house and the heartbeat of *vayikra.* Once we see what He has done for us and as we grasp who He truly is, then our gift becomes an offering and our worship becomes an act of drawing close. The woman drew close that night and touched the feet of the Holy One, poured perfume on the Lord and created an aroma that pleased all of heaven. In a moment of lavish generosity, she showed us all what extravagant sacrifice looks and feels like, for having caught His heart, she now gave her own!

"The result of such 'coming close' is that, after it, we return to the world changed. Renouncing our ownership of something ... we acknowledge God's ownership of the world."[14]

Endnotes

1. Mark 14:3
2. The New Interpreters Dictionary of the Bible – Abingdon Press, 2009, vol.1, p.95
3. Mark 14:3
4. The New Interpreters Dictionary of the Bible, vol.4, p.222
5. John 12:4-6
6. *The Crisis*, Thomas Paine, 23rd December 1776
7. Exodus 30:25; 37:29 and Nehemiah 3:8
8. For example, Leviticus 1:17, 2:9, 3:5 and 4:31
9. Amos 5:21-24
10. Rabbi Jonathan Sacks, *Covenant and Conversation – Leviticus: the Book of Holiness*, Maggid Books & Orthodox Union, 2015, location 1258 (ebook)
11. Rabbi Sacks, *Covenant and Conversation* – location 1229
12. Rabbi Sacks, *Covenant and Conversation* – location 1167
13. Rabbi Sacks, *Covenant and Conversation* – location 1452
14. Rabbi Sacks, *Covenant and Conversation* – location 1258

Chapter 6 – Behaviour's Because

Why did the woman do what she did? What was the reason behind her extravagance? What motivated her to pass the bounds of reason and act in what looked like an absurd, wild, flamboyant or even wasteful way? All behaviour has a *because* ... but what was hers? I'm interested not only in what people do, but why they do what they do. What motivates them to climb that mountain, run that race, serve the poor, go to that country or give themselves to that cause? I've discovered that in finding the reason, the true *because* driving their behaviour, we often start to understand the action itself and the passion within it.

From the biblical narrative, it seems that the Lord too is deeply interested in *why* ... not just what. He is not a tick and flick God. He doesn't just want us to do the right thing, (although it's good to do the right thing), but rather He wants us to do the right thing for the right reasons. As we've observed over the previous four chapters, the actions of the woman were spectacular, to say the least: her *extravagant service* as demonstrated by the tears that washed His feet, followed by the *extravagant statement* of uncovered hair, towelling Him dry. Through her relentless and tender kisses, she offered *extravagant surrender*, climaxing in the *extravagant sacrifice* of expensive perfumed nard! If this was all we had, it would be enough, for these actions surely inspire and provoke us in how to offer our love to the Lord. But the text offers us so much more, for beyond her extravagant behaviour we are made aware of the *because* that fuelled the fire of her passion.

Dr Luke reveals to us that the woman was extravagant to Jesus because He had been extravagant to her! Some have suggested that the actions of the woman were an attempt to find forgiveness from Jesus, but the overwhelming force of the passage tells us the opposite. The extravagance of the woman is not an attempt to find salvation, but rather is a demonstration that salvation has found her. She's not trying to win the favour of Jesus because she has already received His favour! She's not looking for forgiveness; rather her behaviour is expressing it.

How can we be so sure?

Firstly, *the Story*
In verses 41-42, Jesus tells the story of two men who owe the same moneylender some money. One man owes him 500 denarii (1 denarius was the expected salary of a labourer for a day's work) and the other owed him 50 denarii. However, both men were unable to pay, so Jesus reveals that the moneylender cancels the debt of both men. The force and point of the story is in the question Jesus asked at the end:

"Now which of them will love him more?"

From the story, Jesus implies that one man will love the moneylender more because of the extent of the debt cancelled and that their love will flow out of this act of forgiveness. The two men had their debts cancelled and although both were grateful, the implication is that the one who had the biggest debt cancelled would in turn "love the most".

If we directly apply this to the woman, then Jesus is saying that her actions are a result of the fact that she has already had her debt cancelled, and therefore is showing her appreciation to Him. It's interesting that the word translated *forgave the debts* is **charízomai** and has at its heart the idea of a grace gift of mercy and favour. The gift of debt-cancellation was unmerited, yet was given anyway because of the generosity of the one to whom the debt was owed. Paul picks up the same idea when addressing the church in Ephesus:

"Be kind and compassionate to one another, *forgiving* each other, just as in Christ God *forgave* you." (Ephesians 4:32)

Using the same word, Paul reminds the Christian community that their unpayable debt was cancelled because of the grace of God and, therefore, they should behave in the same way towards those who may be in debt to them.

From the story, Jesus is clearly saying, the woman *has already had* her "large" unpayable debt cancelled!

Some have suggested that through this illustration Jesus is implying there are differing grades or levels of sin. Through the image of the "greater" debt and the idea that someone can be forgiven "much", it seems to imply that some sinners are worse than others. Another possible implication is that it's really bad sinners that make the greatest God-lovers and that those who have only sinned a little love a little, while those who have sinned a lot, love a lot. To go down this route is to ignore the context of the story and miss the point Jesus was making, while potentially adding something into this text specifically, and the Bible generally, which isn't there.

But how do we address this concern? Three truths help us understand the heart of what is being said.

Sin is sin

Though there may be different consequences for differing sins, the Bible makes it clear to us that if we break the Law in one area, we've broken it all. Of course, at a societal level there is a huge difference in the impact and consequences of killing someone or cheating on a test – but in the eyes of the Lord, both acts of sin affect our relationship with Him in equal measure. Think of it like this … if you and I sat an exam where the pass mark was 50%, I scored 49% and you scored 20%, both of us would have failed. However, through a perversion that comes out of pride, I might say I still did better than you – or failed less than you did. I might conclude that I failed, but not as badly as you! This is the sort of game people play in their hearts every day – that our "little sins" aren't as bad as really "big sins" and that someone who drives too fast on the roads should never be placed in the same category as someone who blows up a train. But in the eyes of the Lord, sin is sin!

We were powerless to pay our debt (whether big or small)

When it comes to debt, there is one simple reality: if we haven't got the money to pay, in one regard, the size of the debt is irrelevant. If I'm broke, I might only owe £1,000, but it might as well be £1,000,000! The power that debt has over me is not so much in the amount, but whether or not I have the ability to pay. Perhaps you're a homeowner and the mortgage for your house is £100,000. Though that is a huge amount of money, if the monthly payments are being made every month, the debt is being addressed. If, however, I have this mortgage but have lost my job, suddenly the same amount of money has become a tyrannical master.

The Bible makes is clear that the "wages of sin is death"[1] and that we did not have the means to pay the sin-debt we owed. I became a follower of Jesus when I was eight years old and some might argue my sin-debt was relatively small compared to the murderer in prison, but I was powerless to pay that small debt and therefore was under the rulership of darkness. Without the grace-gift of God's debt-cancellation I would have remained in debt, unable to pay and lost for all eternity! Compared to Simon, the woman may have been regarded as having a greater sin-debt, but as the story of Jesus illustrates, neither of them had the power to pay!

Awareness rather than amount

From the story Jesus is not suggesting that big sinners make better lovers of God. Rather, the implication is one of awareness of the extent of the cancellation, rather than the amount itself. If we conclude that sin is sin, no matter what it is, and that sin creates for us an unpayable debt, then it follows that it is not about the size, but rather, the cancellation of the debt that really matters. That way, someone who has had a £50 debt cancelled can be as grateful and passionate as someone who has had £500,000 cancelled. Our focus should not be on how much was cancelled, but on the simple, glorious and mind-blowing fact that it was cancelled!

Secondly, *His Statement*

"Therefore, I tell you, her many sins have been forgiven..." (v47)

From the construction of this language, we are left in no doubt as to where the woman stands. Forgiveness here is used in the perfect passive indicative tense – which tells us that the woman received this as a completed action in the past, resulting in her current condition. From this it is clear, "she has been forgiven."

Why then does Jesus pronounce, "Your sins are forgiven" later in verse 48? This suggests He's forgiving her at that moment. Both the word for forgiveness and the tense here are identical to verse 47. This might then read, "Your sins have been and remain forgiven." Perhaps Jesus makes this statement not only to show that she is forgiven, but that He is the One who has forgiven her – hence the reaction of Simon's guests in verse 49. Either way, it seems clear that Jesus' public pronouncement in verse 48 was simply a confirmation and affirmation of what He referenced in verse 47. No one in the room would be in any doubt from the words of Jesus as to whether the woman was forgiven or not.

Thirdly, *Her Status*

"Your faith has saved you; go in peace." (v50)

I love the power of the words in this simple statement.

Faith – from this word, Jesus made it clear, just in case folks in the room weren't so sure, that it was her faith that saved her, not her actions. Her actions were the *expression* of her faith, not the *means* to it. Jesus has already made it clear from the preceding parable that nothing she could have done could have cancelled the debt she owed. Having been touched by the Word, faith was created enabling the woman to believe and be saved.

Saved – the word translated saved here is *sốzō* and points to the idea of deliverance and bringing to wholeness and safety. It occurs approximately fifty-four times in the Gospels and of the instances where it is used, fourteen relate to deliverance from disease or demon possession.[2] In twenty instances the inference is to the rescue of physical life from some impending peril or instant death,[3] while the remaining twenty times[4] the reference is to spiritual salvation.[5] By using this word, Jesus is describing something life-changing and dramatic that has already happened to the woman. Her life has been revolutionised and made whole by this act of grace.

Go – the word translated go here is ***poreúomai***, meaning to "move from one place to another, to move or to go". This is the same word used by Jesus to the woman caught in the act of adultery in John 8, when He proclaims,

"Neither do I condemn you … *go* now and leave your life of sin." (v12)

I love the image here – that having been transformed, having had her life turned the right way round, Jesus wants her to move *from* something, move *into* something and move *because* of something. For the woman in John 8, He wants her to move from her life of sin into the new opportunity that His actions have created for her. For the woman in our story, having been saved and had her unpayable debt cancelled, she is being encouraged to move into something new, greater, bigger and better.

Peace – the word translated peace here is ***eirēnē***, pointing to a "state of well-being and concord". In the Septuagint (the Greek translation of the Hebrew Bible) *eirēnē* is the usual translation of shalom (*šālôm*), expressing the idea of soundness, wholeness, completeness and peace. At one level, Jesus might simply be offering the woman a farewell comment – "Go and be well, go in God's wholeness and blessing" – but at another level, I believe Jesus is sending this woman into the life-giving wholeness which comes out of His forgiveness. Having been in the brokenness of her sin-debt, she is now set free to live life as the Lord originally intended her to live it. She has not simply been set free to live her own life, but to live the life He has for her.

Paul sums this up magnificently when he concludes:

"For it is by grace you have been saved, through faith – and this not from yourselves, it is the gift of God – not by works so that no on can boast. For we are God's workmanship, created in Christ Jesus to do good works, which God prepared in advance for us to do." (Ephesians 2:8-10)

In summary we might say,

Grace – faith – works!

Grace makes faith possible and faith makes works powerful!

Having received grace and been saved through the faith given to us, we can now go on to become all that we were originally intended to be by Him. We can live as the workmanship of His hands, experiencing His life-giving salvation and His hope-making peace. We have the opportunity to *become* due to His grace-gift to us. This then becomes our *because* as we seek to live for Him.

The woman gave extravagantly because she had become aware of how extravagant the Lord had been to her. I love how Vine puts it when he says, "Love can be known only from the actions it prompts."[6] These are the actions of passionate love in response to the extravagant grace and mercy of the Lord. Having freely received she now freely gives. The reason she acted so extravagantly was because Jesus had been so extravagant to her and she knew it. Therefore, the love she pours out so flamboyantly is the result of God's extravagant flamboyance in her life.

Yet, over the many years I've been a follower of Jesus, I have seen my own passion for Him ebb and flow, as well as that of those around me. How could that happen? If what happened to this woman has happened to us, how could it be possible to lose our zest and passion and allow our hearts to become cold? My journey has taught me that there are three great enemies to the heart of extravagance, seen also through the struggles of an early Christian community.

In the book of Revelation, Jesus rebuked a local church of believers because their passion for Him had cooled. These were good people, doing good work and, on the surface of it, making a difference to their world, but Jesus said:

"Yet I hold this against you: You have forsaken the love you had at first." (Revelation 2:1-7 (v4))

In the words He then speaks to them, the three enemies are highlighted:

The first is Focus

"...the love you had at *first*." (v4)

Later in trying to help them find a way back He says,

"...do the things you did at *first*." (v5)

Somehow they had lost their singular focus of Him and it had drifted onto something else. Ironically, as the passage suggests, their focus was not so much on the Lord of the work, but on the work of the Lord. In the early verses they are commended for their deeds, hard work and perseverance, their stance against evil and their ability to work through hardship. It seems this became the focus of their passion and, over time, subtly (because it never happens quickly), program became more important than His presence. Work substituted the call of worship.

Over the years leaders have backslidden while still filling the pulpit, and good people have grown cold while still attending their local church. It is easy to become intoxicated by the program and draw a deep sense of self-worth and joy from our work, but the danger is that these things start to take our focus and therefore our love. Ephesus was a great Christian community, yet the fire of its love had gone out over time, while at the same time doing all the right things. Rarely is passion destroyed or stolen by a single moment or one particular act. Experience has taught me that it is often and more usually wooed away by a gradual shift of focus from Him to something or someone else. Our heart will follow our eyes and once our focus starts to change, our passion will soon follow! *When we lose focus, extravagance always diminishes.*

The second is Forgetfulness.
"Consider how far you have fallen…"
The word translated "consider" here is *mnēmoneúō*, and means "to remember, call to mind or to exercise the memory". Jesus is asking them to remember because they have forgotten. I don't believe they had forgotten in the sense of wiped from their memory, but somehow the reality of what Jesus had done for them and the amazing story of their salvation had been pushed to the back of their minds. In asking them to consider how far they've fallen, the Lord is asking them to remember what they had and where they came from. If they can remember, everything will be different.
David put it so beautifully:
"Praise the Lord, oh my soul, and forget not all His benefits…" (Psalm 103:2)
He then goes on to list the benefits, reminding himself and

all who are listening, how good the Lord has been and, by implication, how good He will be again!

When we forget what He has done, our own thoughts, or someone else's interpretation of our past, will fill the void. A different version of events will start to dominate our narrative and, before we know it, we'll struggle to recall the stories of His power, provision and providence in our lives.

I remember sitting with a young couple who were struggling in their relationship. At that moment, in truth I wasn't sure what to say or how to help them. Then in my desperation I received a flash of inspiration and I asked them these questions: "What attracted you to each other when you first met? What was it about the other that caused you to fall in love with them?" Slowly, the session began to change as their focus shifted and they started to remember the good times, some funny things about each other, but most of all the uncluttered simplicity of the original love they had for one another.

We quickly forget that's why we have to work hard at remembering. At a simple level, the Bible is a book of remembrance, helping us to go forward by looking back. *When we forget, extravagance always diminishes.*

The third is Familiarity

"…you have forsaken…"

The word translated "forsaken" here is **aphiēmi**, a word sometimes translated "forgiven". It's made up of two words, *apó* – "from" and *hiēmi* – "to send". The idea here (as in forgiveness)[7] is to send something away. Perhaps we've heard the saying, "familiarity breeds contempt", and that is so true. The reason this happens is because we fail to be intentional around the key issues of our lives, allowing them to become routine, ordinary and matter-of-fact. In reality, we've sent their importance away from us, thus giving us permission to handle precious things as common and holy things as ordinary.

Familiarity invades the world of faith as easily as any other, if we allow it to. The Bible becomes a book, worship a song, a sermon becomes a talk, and local church an option. We compromise on issues we never would have before and the spark of specialness has gone because the Lord is just one of many other important things in our world.

I knew a young man who always referred to his parents by their first names. This annoyed me, as I found it too familiar and it was something I never did with my own mum or dad. To me it seemed disrespectful and familiar in all the wrong ways. However, the young man's father tragically died. Strangely, at his funeral he referred to him as "Dad" and not once by his name. Sometimes it's not until we haven't got something or someone that we realise what we had. But it doesn't have to be that way; we can learn to appreciate what we have while we have it and we can honour the holy in our world now. We can maintain a love-filled passion, provided we keep the enemy of familiarity at bay.

When we become familiar, extravagance diminishes.

Ephesus was a great church, but they lost their way. Somehow their focus changed over time. They pushed to the back of their minds the stuff that should have always been at the forefront, and they became casual with the sacred and the special. If it can happen to them, it can happen to us. It's hard to believe that the passion we see in Luke 7 could evaporate and become cold and indifferent. We must fight to keep the fire burning, so that our behaviour never loses its "because" and extravagance for Him remains our way of life.

Take a moment to reflect on the following:

Re-focus: you had an unpayable debt
"Neither of them had the money to pay him back…" (Luke 7:42)
We could never have paid the debt we owed, but through the extravagant sacrifice of Jesus on the cross and His resurrection from the dead, our debt has been paid, granting us forgiveness, freedom and unfettered access to the presence of God.
Where's your focus?
Is it on program or *presence*?
Is it on work or *worship*?

Remember your new account is now full
"Your faith has saved you; go in peace." (Luke 7:50)
Not only did God's grace wipe out the debt, but the righteousness of Christ has been credited to our account. That means in spiritual terms we are beyond billionaires, that we have been blessed "with every spiritual blessing in Christ Jesus"[8] and all of this by the grace, goodness and generosity of the Lord.
How's your memory?
Recall how He saved you and the difference this made to the direction and quality of your life?
If you have some, get your old journals out and read the testimonies of goodness you recorded there. If you don't have journals, grab a blank piece of paper or create a new note on your tablet or phone, and start to list all the good gifts God has given to you.

Renew your zeal for the Lord
Paul said, "Rejoice in the Lord always. I say it again: Rejoice!"

(Philippians 4:4)

I'm a Liverpool supporter and in recent years our form hasn't reflected our history or our expectations. It's fair to say there have been more disappointments than triumphs. But I've been supporting them since 1974 and I'm not going to quit now. Recently I met a guy who connects to me on social media and we started chatting about football. He said something that struck me. He observed that when Liverpool was playing I was always talking them up, giving them my support. He said, "When it comes to Liverpool you're an eternal optimist." I suppose I am, although I don't always feel like it.

The point is this: my zeal for Liverpool doesn't depend on the result – I'm just passionate for the team and, whatever happens, I'll always be a follower. So it is with the Lord. There are times, mostly every day, when we have to make the decision to celebrate Him whether we feel like it or not, whether we think He's worthy of it or not, and whether anything of breakthrough seems to be happening or not. Part of the process of renewing our zeal for Him is talking Him up; it is "bigging up" His name, and as we've seen already in this book, exalting Him in our own mind and heart, regardless of the result!

What's your confession?

Learn to sing when you're not winning.

Speak out the promises the Lord has made over your life.

Exalt His name over your circumstances.

Declare His goodness for all to hear.

The extravagance illustrated by the woman in our story is glorious, and it's hard to imagine that such passion could ever dissipate. But it can and it will, unless we protect the *because* at the heart of our journey. When a change of focus, forgetfulness or familiarity begins to infect our *because*, our extravagance will soon diminish and eventually disappear. When we remember how extravagant He has been to us, then we will always be extravagant to Him!

Endnotes

1. Romans 6:23

2. Matthew 9:21, 22; Mark 3:4; 5:23, 28, 34; 6:56; 10:52; Luke 6:9; 8:36, 48, 50; 17:19; 18:42; John 11:12

3. Matthew 8:25; 14:30; 16:25; 27:40, 42, 49; Mark 8:35; 15:30, 31; Luke 9:24, 56; 23:35, 37, 39; John 12:27

4. Matthew 1:21; 10:22; 19:25; 24:13, 22; Mark 8:35; 10:26; 13:13, 20; 16:16; Luke 7:50; 8:12; 9:24; 13:23; 18:26; 19:10; John 3:17; 5:34; 10:9; 12:47

5. Zodhiates, S. (2000). *The complete word study dictionary: New Testament* (electronic ed.). Chattanooga, TN: AMG Publishers.

6. W.E.Vine, *Exposition Dictionary of New Testament Words*, Zondervan, 1952, Vol.III, p21.

7. For example, it's the same word used by Jesus for forgive in Luke 23:34

8. Ephesians 1:3

Chapter 7 – The Worst of Places ... The Best of Places

We've seen what the woman did through her extravagant *service*, *statement*, *surrender* and *sacrifice*, and in our previous chapter we observed the reason she did what she did. She was extravagant to Him because He had been extravagant to her. But there is a final thread in this tapestry that deserves our consideration before we move on from her actions – namely the *place* in which her extravagance took place. What she did and why she did it must be understood in the context of *where* she did it. The place of her extravagance adds even more value to an already expensive gift, revealing yet more of the heart of the giver and the extent to which she was prepared to go for the One she loved!

When we add the content of the gift to the cause for which it was given and the context in which it was offered, we begin to catch a glimpse of the depths from which extravagance flows and the lengths it is prepared to go. The text leaves us in no doubt as to where this event took place: "...He [Jesus] went to the Pharisee's house and reclined at the table" (v36), and for the woman this was both the worst of places and the best of places! As we look at little closer at the place we learn a little bit more about the power of her actions.

It was a public place – she stepped out

Luke 7:35 not only concludes the story of John the Baptist's question about the type of Messiah Jesus was but, in Dr Luke's thinking, it connects his readers naturally to our story, which begins in verse 36, when Jesus declared,

"But wisdom is proved right by all her children." This statement was not only to help us look back on the previous episode, but look forward to the next one.

In Matthew's version of John's question, the verse reads,

"But wisdom is proved right by her deeds." (Matthew 11:19)

There is no contradiction here as both verses are essentially saying the same thing in slightly different ways. In Matthew it is action that proves wisdom right, whereas in Luke it is "her children" that proves wisdom – implying that anyone who does deeds that prove wisdom, is in fact a "child of wisdom". The word translated "proves" is **dikaióō,** and means "to justify", but in this context it points to the idea of "drawing out what is within or desired". This presents us with a beautiful picture: that we know the children of wisdom because their actions draw out what is within wisdom, or that which wisdom desires.

This verse then looks back and points forward. When people looked at John they said he had a demon because of his extreme behaviour, and when they observed Jesus they said He was a "glutton and a drunkard, a friend of tax collectors and sinners".[1] However, whatever the people thought of their actions, Jesus made it clear that both His and John's behaviour was proving wisdom right, and that those who accepted their message were wise indeed! Leaving verse 35 and entering the story of the woman in verse 36, there are two possible ways to understand her actions in the light of this verse. The first is that she is wise, because she embraced "the glutton and the drunkard" and saw wisdom in His actions. Regardless of what others said, she had opened her heart and allowed the truth of the "friend of sinners" to enter in, transforming her life. In accepting His wisdom she had become wise herself. The second is that her own actions are proving wisdom right and that in fact she is a "child of wisdom" because her extravagance drew out what resided within wisdom's heart. Though Simon's intellectual prowess far outstripped her ability, it seems her offering showed she was the wisest person in the room.

I believe that both meanings apply to the woman – that she was wise because of *who* she received and wise because of *what* she gave.

However, we only know this because the woman went from private to public with her extravagance. She stepped out into a public place, where all could see, and demonstrated wisdom's virtue. As we've seen already in chapter two, Simon's house was both private and public, in that although it was his house, the culture allowed for public access to the event, thus making it a cross-over point. When the woman stepped out that night, she picked the most public of places to do so, the house of a prominent pharisee. Within twenty-four hours, everyone in her town would know what she had done. Her actions would have been powerful even within the privacy of her own home, but in such a public arena they proclaimed to one and all the depth of her conversion and the strength of her conviction!

John records the journey Nicodemus faced. Like Simon, he was a pharisee and a member of the Jewish ruling council. He started his journey in private (John 3:1-21), and later attempted to stand up for Jesus when his peers set out to destroy Him (John 7:50-51). But it was at the death of Jesus that he truly stepped out for what he believed and in a dramatic way identified himself with Jesus and, by implication, declared himself to be a follower of Jesus (John 19:38-42). Like the woman, Nicodemus had to go from private to public in order to prove wisdom right and show himself to be a child of wisdom. Though it may start in private, it cannot remain there. At some point, extravagance must go public to show the world the depth of our conversion and the strength of our conviction!

I had known Dawn for two weeks when I plucked up the courage to ask her out on a cold October Friday evening. (Technically, I asked her to go for a walk, even though she had a broken leg, and she said "Yes", so that counts in my book). In reality I was desperate. I hadn't eaten or slept properly for about a week because I couldn't stop thinking about her, so my logic dictated that even if she turned me down, at least I could start enjoying food again. Remarkably (and it still blows my mind), she not only said yes that night, but she eventually became my wife and has become my best friend.

However, when I asked her out, we had to keep it a secret. Dawn was a 1st year and I was a 3rd year in Bible college at the time, and although we weren't doing anything illegal or immoral, it was certainly on the wrong side of what was expected! As the weeks passed, I came to the realisation that I was in love with her, but I couldn't tell a soul … and it was killing me. I wanted to tell everyone I knew. I wanted to ring my parents and tell them I'd met the woman I was going to marry. I wanted to be able to go for walks with her and hold her hand and show her off and do normal couple stuff, but I couldn't! Those few months leading up the Christmas holidays were challenging – not because I couldn't keep a secret, but because *I didn't want to.* What relief I experienced when I told my mum and dad that Christmas and showed my family her picture for the first time. Soon the world could know, and would know!

Though some things start in private, they must go public. If my passion to and for Dawn only ever remained private, I'm not sure it would be complete. I wanted, and still want, my children and my world to know how much Dawn has changed my heart and enriched me as a person. She is my helper, my friend and my confidante. She completes me and makes me look better than I am. I want her to know I know that, but I want my world to know that I know that. My extravagance for her must go public to show the world the depth of my conversion and the strength of my conviction!

How's your public extravagance for Him?

Someone may challenge me by responding that "faith is a private affair..." but it's not. It never has been and it never will be. True love and faith must not and cannot be kept under lock and key, they need to go public; they need to let the world know the depth of conversion and the strength of conviction. Without actions, wisdom is a concept and an idea, but through actions, wisdom can be seen through her children. It's good to be passionate in private, but at some point it has to go public. The journey from private to public is not always an easy one, but it is a necessary one.

That night, when the woman in our story went from private to public and stepped out, her extravagance turned a public place into a prophetic platform! Even though she did not say a word, her actions spoke forth to her world of her love for Jesus and her desire to serve Him.

It was a hostile place – she stepped up
The public space belonged to Simon, who we know was a

pharisee. As a "separated one", Simon was committed to understanding, teaching and living the Law. For him, the Torah was at the heart of everything, and though it is easy for some to criticise such religious zeal, men like Simon were serious about God, His word and His ways. As part of the outworking of their worship of God, the Pharisaic community (though not exclusively) demonstrated a relentless passion for purity. A glance at the Gospels and we see their commitment to purity rules around food and the vessels containing food and liquid.[2] They were concerned about purity when eating food, especially the issue of clean and unclean hands.[3] They had purity regulations around corpses and tombs,[4] and the importance of the Temple.[5] They were serious about tithing[6] and observing the Sabbath and holy days,[7] as well as seeing themselves as guardians on key areas of morality. So of all the places that this woman could decide to step out, this was probably one of the most hostile environments for her to do so, within the context of her culture! She was at the opposite end of the spectrum to everything Simon believed in and aspired to. She was a sinner and he was not; she was dirty and he was clean; she was most certainly in the world, while he was working hard to separate himself from it.

Hostility can range from general unfriendliness to aggressive opposition, with every possible scenario in between. Though no one said anything directly to the woman, we can but imagine the holes being burnt into her back by every set of religious eyes laid upon her. Had she asked Simon for permission to do what she was doing, it would not have been given in a thousand lifetimes, so she weathered the unspoken hostility around her and stepped up to minister to Jesus. That evening extravagance took her faith from a place of comfort to confrontation. Her actions, at best, put her on the radar of the religious and, at worst, made her a target for some form of retaliation or censure. Stepping out in public meant she had to step up in a hostile place as her courage gave her conviction a face!

I don't get to see my beloved Liverpool play live that often, so when I do, I tend to try and savour every moment of it. I remember back in November 2010 going to watch them play European opposition. The team in question was Napoli and it was expected to be a close game. I managed to get a ticket in the world famous Kop and the ground was packed with almost 45,000 spectators. The Napoli supporters were positioned at the Anfield Road end of the ground, directly opposite the Kop, and thousands of them were singing and making as much noise as they could.

On the 28th minute of the first half, Napoli scored through a strike by Ezequiel Lavezzi, which stunned the Liverpool supporters and sent the Napoli supporters wild ... and wild they went. However, something happened at that moment that I will never forget. Somehow, a few hundred Napoli supporters had managed to get tickets for areas of the stadium reserved only for Liverpool fans, and when their team scored, they all started jumping up and down, swinging their scarfs around their heads – which was a very brave (or stupid) thing to do. My eyes were drawn away from the thousands of Napoli supporters celebrating together, to these few, scattered, courageous souls, standing out so conspicuously! It was because they were in the wrong area, waving the wrong colour scarfs that I noticed them all the more – pinpricks of light blue in a sea of red.

At the moment when their team scored, they decided to step up and show the world around them where their allegiance lay and how much they loved their team, even if it was the last thing they ever did! I can happily report that during that evening, no Napoli supporters were harmed in the making of this illustration and that Liverpool went on to win the game 3-1, thanks to a Steven Gerrard hat-trick! However, I still remember their courage. They stood out because they stepped up in a hostile context.

Solomon tells us,

"The fear of man will prove to be a snare…" (Proverbs 29:25)

The anxiety that comes from the uncertainty of how people will react to our behaviour can create a snare or form a noose, thus restricting our movements and actions. Snares are typically wire nooses that are used to trap animals in cruel and inhuman ways, and they are designed to do at least three things:

They are designed to capture

The primary reason anyone sets a snare is to catch something, whether it be a fox, a badger or a rabbit. It is set in such a way that any animal that strays into it will be quickly and ruthlessly captured. As an owner of two beautiful Dachshunds, Pepperoni and Salami, I'm often fearful that in their zest to chase rabbits, or anything else that moves in the woods, they will be victims of illegal snaring, because once in, it's hard to get any animal out.

As a teenager, I had a crush on a girl who lived around the corner. Her name was Sandra. She was a year older than me and although a bit of a tomboy, she was feminine enough to cause my heart rate to rise every time I saw her. I wanted to ask Sandra out for over a year, but I never did. There was even a rumour that she wanted me to ask her out, but I never did! I dreamed of asking her out, but I never did. I was terrified that she would say no and I would be the butt of jokes in the neighbourhood. Captivated by fear, the opportunity passed me by. Now you know why asking Dawn to go for a walk on a cold October evening, even though she had a broken leg, was for me, such an achievement ... one of my greatest!

They are designed to restrict

The snare doesn't just capture, it restricts. I know that sounds like the same thing, but once captured by the snare, any further movement of the animal causes the snare to tighten its hold on the beast. The aim of the tightening noose is to stop the animal moving at all, so it will surrender to its fate.

My mum has managed to get to all of my graduations except one ... my first one! Back in 1987 when I graduated from Bible college, my mum didn't make it because she was afraid of flying. Someone told her that being on a plane would affect her claustrophobia and she believed them. Every time she thought about getting on a plane, the thought of a claustrophobic episode held her back. However, she has overcome the fear and since then she's travelled to different parts of the world, including the graduation services for my Masters and PhD ... all on a plane! But when restricted by fear, the opportunity passed her by.

They are designed to injure

Tragically, snares don't only capture and restrict, but in most cases they injure and destroy. Thankfully, this thought doesn't come with pictures, but some of the injuries I've seen as a result of snares are horrific! When people set snares it's with a view to eventually killing whatever has been caught, but in many cases, the captured beasts are already dead as a result of the injuries produced by the snare.

Fear has a nasty habit of cutting into our hearts and digging into our confidence. Broken relationships, powerful words, insecurities and memories of past failure, can all injure our souls and leave a scar. Over the years I've met beautiful people who believe they are ugly and gifted people who believe they are useless, trapped and now injured by the words and actions of others. Just as the "sinner" label could have stood in the way of the woman, words and events can snare us, tightening their grip on our hearts. Injured by fear, the opportunity can pass us by.

However, I'm so glad that Solomon didn't just leave us the first half of his Proverb, but he added a glorious second phrase:

"...but whoever trusts in the Lord is kept safe."

To be kept safe here is to be shielded from injury, danger, destruction or damage. Everything the snare is designed to do is countermanded when we trust in the Lord. His love has the power to emancipate, liberate and heal, for it is through His perfect love that all fear is cast out and we can be all we were designed to be![8]

Had the woman given into the fear of that hostile place, then the story of her extravagance would never have been written, Jesus' feet would have remained dirty, and the room would never have smelled the perfume of worship. It is hard to think of a more hostile place for the woman to do what she did, and yet she did it, stepping up in the face of fear, turning a hostile room into a holy place!

I don't know what your world looks like, but anything that seeks to capture, restrict or injure you represents a "hostile place". It may be a physical place, or it may reside in words or thoughts, but it is the enemy of extravagance. It is almost impossible to be extravagant when fear reigns. That's why, like the woman, the Lord wants His love to reign in you. When love entered the woman's world it drove fear out, and when fear left, her extravagance was able to turn a hostile room into a holy place. Don't allow hostility to keep your perfume in the bottle. Let your extravagance set its holy perfume free!

It was a demanding place – she stepped forward

Not only did the woman step out and step up that night, but in a very real way, she stepped forward. Up until the moment of her offering, she had been a recipient of Jesus' grace and a benefactor of His mercy and love. Her experience had been one in which Jesus had done all the giving, cancelling her debt and setting her on the path of peace. The easiest thing in the world would have been for the woman to "take the money and run". After all, she would not be the first or last to do so. Jesus was accustomed to the fact that the crowds liked it when He gave, but were not always as happy when He started challenging them with the call of His message. By the time Jesus left the earth thousands had taken what He had to offer without giving anything back in return – such is the magnificence of His grace and the selfishness of the human heart!

However, this was the night the woman journeyed from being a consumer to a contributor. Having freely received from Him, she decided that she was going to freely give to Him. In the context of what she gave and where she gave it, this was indeed a demanding moment, and one that cost her dearly, but as she stepped forward that night, the demanding place became for her a defining place. In her action of extravagance she went from a blessed woman to a believing woman, from a benefactor to a blesser, and from a freeloader to a follower. Her extravagance defined her as one of His disciples.

I love how Amy Carmichael, the famous missionary who spent most of her ministry life in India, put it when she said, "You can give without loving, but you cannot love without giving."

How true this is. Giving can be casual, but extravagance cannot. Giving sometimes comes out of duty, but extravagance flows out of passion. Giving can be forced by guilt or pressure, but extravagance runs free. Giving can feel like a "have to" thing, whereas extravagance is always a "want to" thing!

Simon gave that night, but the woman was extravagant. Simon did just enough, while the woman did more than enough. Simon did his basic duty, while the woman's actions were pure desire.

That's why extravagance is both demanding and defining. What, why, how and where we give will say something to God and to our world, but it will also say something about us. A decision of extravagance can change everything because essentially it transforms us from being a consumer to a contributor; having freely received we are determined to freely give!

I remember the first time I danced (jumped up and down really) in a worship service. No one did it where I was and no one was doing it at that moment, yet I wanted to lift my hands in worship; I wanted to shout out His goodness over my life; and I wanted to jump up and down as an expression of my thanksgiving to Him. My heart was racing while my head was filled with doubts and fears, with the words that people might say if I did it. My heart was burning for Him but my eyes were fixed on the people around me. I allowed the place to drive the agenda instead of my love and passion for the Lord. Then I had a simple revelation: "Who am I doing this for?" It wasn't for me, and it certainly wasn't for the people around me, rather, it was for Him. As I answered my unspoken question I found myself dancing (or jumping or something), but as I did so, joy filled my heart and energy rushed through my body. Something changed in me that night, not because I jumped, but because I refused to allow the place to determine my agenda for worship. I've never looked back!

It was the worst of places and the best of places in which the woman acted so extravagantly. In such a public place she stepped out and openly expressed her conviction about Jesus. In the hostile place she stepped up and demonstrated enormous courage to live beyond the fear-snare, and in the demanding place she stepped forward and made a commitment to not just remain a consumer, but become a contributor. Her extravagance turned a public place into a prophetic platform, as conviction triumphed over comfort. Her extravagance transformed a hostile space into a holy sanctuary, as love conquered fear and her extravagance changed a demanding moment into a defining experience. Having been set free, she would now follow!

Extravagance doesn't always find the perfect place or can't wait for the perfect moment, but it has the power, if let loose, to transform any place and redefine any moment.

Endnotes

1. Luke 7:33-34
2. Matthew 23:25-26
3. Mark 7:1-5
4. Matthew 23:27-28
5. Matthew 23:16-22
6. Matthew 23:23
7. Mark 2:23-28; Luke 14:1-16 & John 9:1-34
8. 1 John 4:18

Chapter 8 – Not Everyone Gets It

So far, our eyes have been on the extravagant actions of the woman, and over the last seven chapters I've attempted to slow this episode down to a frame-by-frame view, giving us (I hope) both a panoramic perspective as well as the power of the detail. Though her extravagance dominates the picture, she is not the only person in the frame. Her actions initiate a chain reaction, setting Simon and Jesus on a collision course. The response of both men now becomes the focus of Dr Luke's attention, revealing not only what they thought about the woman, but throwing a light on their own hearts and attitudes. In the next few moments of the story we see the paradox created by "grace and truth" – a running theme in the ministry of Jesus. In the same room that night we have inclusion and exclusion, compassion and challenge, opportunity and opposition. We observe the beauty of the gospel and the brutality of religion. Bridging the gap between these two worlds is Jesus, offering acceptance to the woman while seeking to create a path of grace for Simon. If Simon responds positively and humbly to Jesus, he too can find the heart of God and the joy of extravagance, but if he reacts negatively and self-righteously, he will find himself trapped in a tower of intolerance and miss the offer of grace.

As we now examine the reaction of Simon to the woman's behaviour, we must be careful not to fall into the very attitudinal trap which we may deem him guilty of. Remember, Simon was a good man and he loved God passionately. His commitment to the Bible was unquestioned and he lived his life in a way that he believed brought pleasure to God. So before we judge him, remember there is a *Simon in us all* and, if we're honest, the self-righteous pharisee lurking somewhere within us is more influential than we dare admit. The longer we follow Jesus, the more knowledge we accumulate, and the further away we get from the moment when our debt was cancelled and Jesus met us for the first time, the more prone we are to believe our own propaganda and make dangerous assumptions that we are (even if just a little) better than the people around us. It becomes easier to look down our self-righteous noses at a broken world and make assumptions on all we see.

Personally, I have to fight the pharisee within me every day. I'm better than I've ever been (I think), but on the days when I hope *Simon* has moved out of my heart, he has a nasty habit of gatecrashing my inner world and dragging me back to his graceless domain. I don't want to live there. I don't want the pharisee to win … but if I don't identify him and contend with him, in my own weakness and self-deception I convince myself that he's gone, when all the time I know he's in the next room, ready to take control and broadcast his opinion. It's too easy to cast Simon as the baddie of this story, booing him as he enters the stage, but before we boo, beware … he's closer to us all than we think!

There is no doubt that the extravagant actions of the woman irritated Simon. I guess if we could have strapped a blood pressure monitor to the host at that moment, he might have

been admitted to hospital for fear of a stroke or heart attack …
or both! The text shows the evidence of his irritation in four
dramatic ways, revealing his own struggle when confronted
with the woman's *appalling* behaviour, opening for us, a
window into his soul.

He was cynical

"If this man were a prophet He would know who is touching
Him…" (v39)

The text makes it clear that Simon spoke these words in his
own head, in or to himself. Whether it was the shock of the
moment, or the fact that he hesitated and therefore missed the
opportunity to stop the woman, Simon doesn't speak out, but
he speaks nonetheless. Though non-verbal, his words are real
and powerful, unheard by Jesus, the woman and others, but
every word, nuance and accent was heard by heaven.

We can be guilty of playing the "private/public world" game
– the idea that what goes on inside us, unseen and unheard,
doesn't really count, and it's only the stuff that makes it into
the public eye for which we're held accountable. The biblical
narrative rejects categorically any split-world philosophy. As
far as the Lord is concerned we inhabit one-world, which
encompasses the so-called private and public arenas. In God's
world, my thoughts are as real as my words; my desires are as
important as my deeds; and my attitudes are weighed as much
as my activity. Whatever people see or hear (and, of course,
our public behaviour is very important), the inner world is
exposed at all times before the Lord. The *Simon* in us all learns
to modify behaviour to fit any context, while disguising the
true belief of our hearts and distracting our world from it.
Simon's skill at pretence will ensure we accumulate a collection

of masks while permitting our hearts to remain unchanged. In a split-world, the *Simon* within us feeds and thrives, but where one-world reigns, he cannot survive!

If we weren't sure about Simon's attitude towards Jesus, his thoughts give us significant insight. Reading this statement, "If this man were a prophet…" in English, we might want to give Simon the benefit of the doubt and read it in a more positive or compassionate way: "Does Jesus know what's going on here? If He did, He'd stop this." But the construction leaves us in little doubt as to the cynicism within Simon's words, for rather than giving Jesus the benefit of the doubt he's damning Jesus as a prophetic fake. "The sentence expresses an unreal condition in present time, that is, both clauses are regarded as untrue." [1] Therefore, Simon concluded that Jesus was not a prophet and that He did not know who was touching Him and what sort of woman she was.

To be cynical is to be "distrustful of human sincerity or integrity" and this certainly describes Simon's thoughts. Maybe Simon had seen men like Jesus before, charismatic rule-benders who pull a crowd but lack substance, offering the vulnerable the promised land but leaving people lost and broken on the road. After all, Simon was a guardian of the Law and saw himself with a responsibility to discern error and protect God's people from spiritual abuse and exploitation. He suspected Jesus was a fraud and now, before his eyes, he was proved correct!

The gorgeous and tragic irony of this inner-thought was that Jesus the "fake prophet" answered Simon as if he had spoken the words out loud. Look at the text again in verse 40: "Jesus answered him…". But Simon hadn't said anything! Yet, with prophetic insight, Jesus responded to the unspoken cynicism of Simon in an unerring way. Note too, the graciousness of Jesus to Simon, as He refused the temptation to expose him by the letting the room know He knew the thoughts of his host. Instead, he let Simon connect the dots for himself!

Simon's cynicism caused him to see something that wasn't there and miss someone that was. He saw what he wanted to see. Rather than challenging him, the "facts" simply confirmed he was right after all. The pharisee lurking in us often sees the world as we are, rather than how it is. When looking at the world through sunglasses, colours change and reality is distorted, as green becomes brown and bright becomes dull. The *Simon* living within us wants us to believe that we are always (or mostly) right, and sooner or later, the facts will prove this to be so. We fall into the trap of seeing through our own cynical lens, rather than seeing someone or something for what it really is. Our lens has been created by pain, disappointment, success, wealth, poverty, health and sickness, how we've been taught and who taught us … in short, everything in our world has the power to influence the lens through which we see it. Simon saw Jesus through a pharisaic lens and concluded He was a phony and not a prophet. He saw the woman through the lens of his interpretation of the Law and saw a sinner rather than a saint! If we're cynical when it comes to extravagance, the problem may be with how we see the world, rather than how the world is.

He was judgmental

"…and what kind of a woman she is – that she is a sinner." (v39)

Note Simon's conclusion about the woman: "…that she *is* a sinner." He thought of her sinful state as being in the present tense, and yet, having read the whole story, we know, she *was* a sinner – past tense! Simon reasons from what he thinks he knows, but by the time we get to verse 39, his *facts* are already out of date. Yet, based on his facts, he makes a judgment about the woman, condemning her in his own mind. Little did he know that her sin-debt had been cancelled and that the extravagance he now witnessed represented the very heart of worship and the highest call of Torah.

There is, of course, a huge difference between making a judgment and being judgmental. We are encouraged to be spiritual people who also engage our brains, so that we can think through, reason out and come to the right conclusion on the issues before us. No matter how good we are at the process, and though we may get it right many times, if you are anything like me, you will also get things wrong and make mistakes. That's just the joy of being human; some days we look brilliant and other days we struggle to spell brilliant. Part of growing up is learning to discern and judge the difference between what is good or bad and wholesome or nasty. The danger lurks where we allow our judgments to be driven by a judgmental approach or form a judgmental attitude. When that happens we tend to become overly critical, moving beyond the boundary of any reasonable rationale into the place of superiority and arrogance. How tempting this is … and how easy it is to succumb.

He can't get a job...
…because he's lazy.
She's dancing in worship...
…to draw attention to herself.
He missed the appointment...
…because he just doesn't care.

She walked past me without speaking...
...*because she's arrogant.*
They don't give as much as me...
...*because they're not committed like I am.*
Those young people...
...*they are all doing drugs and having sex.*
Those oldies...
...*they are always criticising us young people.*
Black people...
...*they are all the same.*
Muslims...
...*none of them can be trusted.*
Christians...
...*what a bunch of hypocrites.*

No one had to teach us to be judgmental – in a fallen, broken world it comes naturally to us. The tragedy is when we pull God's name into our world-view and give the impression that our thoughts are His and that our conclusions are an echo of His words.

Good judgment relies on getting the right facts on the page before we open our mouths. We all know the pain of that journey. But even if and when we get the facts, whatever they are, we fight the pharisee within that wants to take what we think we know and make conclusions that are neither justified nor necessary. The *Simon* within me wants to tell me the sort of people they are, what they're like because of where they've come from, and what they'll do because of where they stand. *Simon* would have me call saints sinners and see agendas where none exist. It's possible to judge without being judgmental, but the pharisee within us won't be satisfied unless we are doing both! If the *Simon* within us reigns, we'll be experts in our own minds, skilled at pulling others down, but unable to build our world up.

If we're judgmental when it comes to extravagance, let's not just check the accuracy of the facts, let's also have the courage to test the attitude of our hearts!

He was indifferent

"*I suppose* the one who had the bigger debt cancelled." (v43)

When Jesus lets Simon know that He has something to tell him, Simon's response is, at least on the surface, open and eager, "'Tell me, teacher,' he said" (v40). However, by the time Jesus got to the end of His story, Simon, as a clever theologian and one schooled in the art of debate, knew where this story was going and that he had unwittingly walked into the Galilean Rabbi's trap. The killer blow for Simon comes with Jesus' concluding question:

"Now which of them will love him more?" (v42)

Simon knows that Jesus is not talking about the two fictitious characters of His story, but rather, Jesus is drawing the contrast between him and *that woman*. Simon knows the right answer, the only answer, but he has to find a way of saying it without losing face or making the "fake" prophet look good. Note his language: the NIV translators try to capture it with the phrase *"I suppose"*[2]. Plummer describes Simon's words as having an "air of supercilious indifference",[3] although Marshall challenges this by suggesting it is more likely Simon was expressing caution. However, he does agree that Simon realised the game was up and that his answer, "… reluctantly anticipates what follows…".[4] But somehow Simon found a way of acknowledging the Master's story without committing himself to the truth. To leave His listeners in no doubt, Jesus concluded, "You have judged correctly" (v43). Simon was right, but on this occasion he desperately wanted to be wrong!

If I were to put "I suppose" in 21st Century speak, it might be translated "Whatever!" and perhaps accompanied by a casual shrug of the shoulders. This is code for "I don't care" and is to passionate, extravagant people what garlic is to vampires ... replusive! Could it be that the indifferent response of Simon provoked the next part of the story, where Jesus highlights the woman? Is it possible that if Simon had responded with humility that the ending to the story might be have been changed? I suspect from the reaction of Jesus and the uncompromising nature of His words (which we'll see in detail in the next chapter), that He is at best disappointed and at worst angry at Simon's *whatever indifference*. I don't think Simon's indifference was because he did not care, but rather because he did not like the answer. Simon checked out because of the discomfort of the challenge Jesus placed before him. The rules of *his* game had changed and he no longer wanted to play.

The pharisee within us likes it when we are in control, when we are (or we think we are) the cleverest person in the room and our version of reality is the only version under consideration. But that same pharisee will start to get uncomfortable when challenged to reconsider, renegotiate, retreat or completely reboot! The *Simon* in my heart wants to be right and doesn't like the idea that I might be wrong. And, if allowed, my *Simon* comes up with plausible explanations that excuse me from the responsibility of facing up to the reality before me, swallowing my pride and making the changes. When it comes to life in general, this mentality is pretty dangerous, but when it comes to our spiritual journey, our relationship with the Lord and the expression of that love through service to His world, this attitude is catastrophic!

As a serious follower of Jesus it is almost impossible to go a single day without experiencing some level of challenge or discomfort. Every time I pick up the Bible, something gets under my skin and if I am truly engaging with His Church, His called-out community, and the world we are asked to reach, dis-*ease* will be a common and consistent experience. As spiritual people following after Jesus, we live with the unending tension of comfort and challenge. The closer we get to Him the more we see His glory and the more we understand how loved and blessed we are. But the closer we get to Him, the more we see His glory and the more we understand what He wants and the challenge that brings to us!

If we shrug our shoulders with "supercilious indifference" we'll miss an opportunity for growth and change and we'll remain in the small world of our own apparent genius. Jesus' story and question to Simon were not to hurt or embarrass him, but to call him from where he was to where God wanted him to be. Don't ignore discomfort's call or the challenge of change, but with a humble heart embrace the way of extravagance. When we stay where we are, we never stay where we are; rather we shrink and become smaller. But when we have the courage to accept the challenge of extravagance, our world will only get bigger. The *Simon* within us wants to remain the biggest person in the room, but if we embrace extravagance, he'll have to find a new room in which to live.

If we're indifferent when it comes to extravagance, it's a sign our hearts have shrunk and our world is smaller than we think.

He was unmoved

Note, from verse 43, there is no record of Simon speaking again and his words of indifference form his last recorded verbal contribution to the story. In fact, it's his guests who speak up in opposition to Jesus and Simon remains quiet, allowing them to get at his guest, something he should not have permitted them to do. Frustratingly, there is no real indication as to what happened next. Did Simon repent? Did he apologise? Did they throw Jesus and the woman out? How did the evening end? When I get to heaven I hope there is a special section in the media library entitled, "What happened next". There are a few stories in the Bible that intrigue me, not just because of what they say, but also because of what they don't say.

What we do know for sure is that Simon doesn't speak again. That might be because he lost round 1 to Jesus and didn't fancy another, or because he's angry or even because he's offended. According to Dr Luke, Simon shows no interest and does not engage from this moment on in any way. There is no record that Simon acknowledged or accepted the words of Jesus. It seems he stayed on his side of the fence and did not move.

When arrogance (cynical and judgmental), gets together with indifference, one of their children will always be apathy. The original meaning behind the word apathy is "freedom from suffering", which has at its core the nuance of being "without feeling". Apathy in a more recent modern sense carries the idea of being without feeling or passion, to be passionless and careless when it comes to important issues and responsibility. To have no feeling is to be apathetic and this seems like an apt description of Simon's actions in the rest of our story. He doesn't fight Jesus and he doesn't yield to Jesus, rather he just checks out and leaves the floor to Him and anyone else who wants to contribute.

Apathy is a sign that something fundamental isn't working right inside us. When we are "without feeling" for people and things that should matter, or for things that used to matter, that's the clearest indicator that something is breaking or has broken. Apathy doesn't just happen, it's the product of other factors colliding and conspiring in our lives. Often I've noticed that those expressing apathy find a way to blame parts of their world that can't produce apathy in them. We credit our apathy to what other people have or have not done, or to the context of our work or the environment in which we live. However, these cannot produce apathy. They can and do certainly contribute *to* apathy once it is within us, but they do not have the power to conceive it. Lack of feeling on any issue comes from decisions made within our own being in regard to those issues. If I deem someone to be important to me, then apathy will have no room in my heart. If I believe something is of value to me, then I will take care of it and invest into it. If my job is more to me than a paycheck then turning up on time and doing my best are never in question. The apathy expressed by Simon to Jesus and the woman reveals his lack of feeling for both, and he is unmoved because he does not care!

Extravagance and apathy cannot share the same space for they are diametrically opposed to each other. Extravagance is *"passing the bounds of reason, wild, absurd, flamboyant, abundant or even wasteful"*, while apathy is "without feeling" and passionless.

As I was writing this chapter, Liverpool (sorry to mention them again) played Borussia Dortmund in the quarter final of the Europa League, and although they were 3-1 down with 20 minutes to go, they managed to win the game 4-3 with a last minute goal by Dejan Lovren. That night, BBC 5 Live

Sport had a phone in and a young man called Michael, a life-long Liverpool supporter called in, ecstatic about the result. However, he revealed that he'd missed the game because he was at the hospital for the birth of his first child, a son. When asked what he was going to name his son he said without hesitation "Dejan" after the guy who scored the winning goal! For those who love Liverpool FC, that's a great story, but to those who don't even understand football, that's just bonkers! Michael's passion for Liverpool was the fuel for his extravagance in naming his firstborn son Dejan – when you love something so much, *why wouldn't you?* But for those who have no passion for such things, the question rings out, *why would you?*

The pharisee within us will always seek to pour cold water on the extravagance of others, while explaining away our own lack of passion. The pharisee doesn't want to be around passionate people or places that might provoke flamboyant or wild behaviour, because extravagance tends to expose apathy. The *Simon* within me finds an excuse for apathy and rehearses a sensible reason as to why what *that woman* is doing is not for me. *Simon* often explains my apathy away using words like personality, personal preference, upbringing and maturity, and although there's nothing wrong with these words, I must always ensure that they are not a disguise for my apathy or for a heart without feeling and passion.

If we are unmoved when it comes to extravagance, we must have the courage to ask what factors have given birth to our apathy and banish them from our hearts.

Jesus didn't expect Simon to cry tears onto His feet or go out and buy expensive perfume for the occasion, but the actions of the woman did challenge Simon to leave the safety of his comfort and venture into the cause of extravagance.

Unfortunately Simon missed the opportunity and chose to remain an expert in his own world, instead of being extravagant in *His* world.

Endnotes

1. Marshall, H.I., *The Gospel of Luke*, NIGTC, Paternoster Press Ltd, 1978, p309.
2. As does, NLT, RSV and ASV.
3. A, Plummer, *The Gospel According to St. Luke*, The International Critical Commentary, T&T Clark, Fifth edition, 1922, p212.
4. Marshall, *The Gospel of Luke*, p311.

Chapter 9 – The Audience of One

Simon's irritation with the actions of the woman is in stark contrast to the initial passivity of Jesus. As she wets His feet with her tears, unbinds her hair to towel them dry, kisses His feet as the face of a lover, and finally pours very expensive perfumed nard onto them, Jesus, it seems, was unmoved as she served, apparently unnoticed by Him. While she lavished herself on Him, He reclined and, most likely, continued to eat the goodies set before Him by His host, showing no sign of discomfort, disapproval or urgency. Looking at Jesus and observing His casual demeanor during the whole event, one might conclude that such an experience was commonplace, carrying no shock value and demanding no response. Yet, as Simon's world shuddered from the appalling extravagance of the woman, Jesus popped another olive into His mouth. If we left the scene at this moment we might conclude that the woman's risk was in vain and that her extravagance was a spectacular failure. However, as we follow the text, we see the apparent disinterest of Jesus evaporate into one of the most passionate defences of any individual in the whole of the Gospels. As Jesus crossed verbal swords with Simon, we discover *He noticed everything and missed nothing!*

In the previous chapter, I highlighted four expressions of Simon's irritation towards the woman's behaviour, almost all of which were muted within the privacy of his own heart. Jesus also responded to the woman in four ways, but in each case His words were heard and His actions were clear. In contrast to the private disgust of Simon, Jesus' admiration of the woman was unrestricted. His extravagant defence of her was both a challenge and a call to the room, a demonstration of what they should have done and what they could become. Through four simple but intentional responses, Jesus silenced the self-righteousness of His host and amplified the worship of the woman, reminding everyone that the Lord "...opposes the proud but exalts the humble".[1] Let's look at His four responses.

Her extravagance got His attention
"Then He turned toward the woman and said to Simon..." (v44)

Remember the layout of the room? Jesus reclined on His left arm while reaching over with His right hand to eat. As his host reclined facing him, the woman knelt behind Jesus and ministered to His feet. In other words, as the episode began, Jesus had His back to the woman and His face to Simon. However, in a split second all of that changed as Jesus dramatically twisted Himself around so as to look at the woman and therefore put His back to Simon. Jesus turned His face away from His host and put it towards her.

In my western cultural context this might seem like a polite thing to do, to show some form of acknowledgement to someone who is serving, but in the culture of Jesus, this carried an even deeper meaning. To help us with this, let's turn to Numbers 6:24-26, to the *Birkat Kohanim*, or the Priestly Blessing.

"The Lord bless you and keep you; the Lord make His face shine on you and be gracious to you; the Lord turn His face toward you and give you peace."

Note the blessing begins in a rather general way with the declaration that the Lord will bless and keep, followed by two more specific statements, both linked to the face of Yahweh. As the Lord's face "turns" toward us, two spectacular consequences follow, namely grace (favour) and peace. Thus the symbolism of the Lord's face moving towards those He loves was as sure a signal of grace, favour, blessing and peace as the heat of the sun warming the earth. Conversely, any sense of displeasure and judgment might be interpreted as the face of God turning away from His people.[2]

As with the Lord, so this idea found its way into human behaviour. When the face was towards someone, it was generally a sign of acceptance, generosity and blessing, whereas when the face was turned away, it might signify unhappiness or even rejection. So, as we return to our story, we might just have an unfortunate social mishap of Jesus, turning His face towards a "sinful" woman, while turning His back on a "man of God" ... or this could be a deliberate, intentional action of Jesus to say something about, and to, both parties. Remember, Simon's last words to Jesus before He turns are, "I suppose..." Could it be that Jesus is turning away from such an attitude as much as He is turning towards the pure passion of the woman? In that moment, Jesus "makes His face shine" upon the woman and literally, "turns His face" towards her, offering her both the favour and peace of the Lord. At the same time, He turns His face away from Simon, the symbolism of which would have been clearly understood by him in the light of the moneylender story. If we are in any doubt of Jesus' intention, He adds insult to injury by speaking to Simon while looking at the woman. He may have been forgiven a social *faux pas* with the turn, but when He speaks to Simon with His face to the woman and His back to His host, something is being communicated in actions beyond the words spoken. Jesus' back is turned to "supercilious indifference" while His face is turned towards extravagant passion.

Humble extravagance will always get the Lord's attention. He doesn't always respond to the most expensive, but He does *turn* towards our best.[3] He doesn't always respond to the biggest or the most, but He does *turn* to something that truly cost us.[4] I am not suggesting, of course, that the Lord's favour is earned, because at the very heart of the definition of grace is an understanding that it is unmerited. However, I do believe that we can pleasure the heart of the Lord; that we can do things with a purity of motive and with no personal agenda or strings attached that causes the face of the Lord to turn towards us in an expression of favour and peace beyond that which, as children of God, we might normally expect. Paul continuously expresses grace and peace as almost a covenant right in his letters to local churches, often beginning and ending with this theme. It is remarkable how often he declares the "grace and peace" of the Father over those who believe. Yet, even though we have this expectation as the norm, Paul also shows that the Lord responds, or turns, towards extravagance.

When writing to Corinth, Paul said,

"Each of you should give what you have decided in your heart to give, not reluctantly or under compulsion, for God loves a cheerful giver. And God is able to bless you abundantly, so that in all things at all times, having all that you need, you will abound in every good work." (2 Corinthians 9:7-8)

Note this: the Lord doesn't want a forced offering, but rather one that comes from the heart, and it seems that when the heart is *cheerful* about the giving, the Lord then responds with lavish extravagance. The word cheerful is *hilarós* and simply means "joyous, happy and cheerful". However, the context doesn't just suggest happy or carefree, in fact, quite the opposite. Paul is pointing here to an extravagant heart attitude that finds expression in a generous gift. This cheerfulness is not superficial or frivolous, but is itself rooted in a dynamic revelation and conviction that the Lord deserves our best. Our extravagance will always get His attention and turn His face!

Her extravagance got His allegiance
"Do you see this woman?" (v44)

I can almost hear Simon think, "Is that a trick question?" How could he miss the woman who was defiling his home and ruining his evening? The woman who had highjacked his planned *chat* with Jesus? Simon was trying not to look at her – he just wanted her out! Yet, by these simple words, Jesus forced His host and the room to focus and look at the offending individual. However, Jesus knew that Simon and his friends could see her, no matter how much they tried not to look, so why say it and state the obvious? Jesus' question wasn't so much asking Simon to look at her, but letting Simon know that *He* was looking at her, that He could see her and was aligning Himself with her. In a room where she had no friends, Jesus wanted Simon to know that at this moment He had become her friend and would defend her cause.

Throughout the Scriptures the Lord was sometimes given a

name by those who encountered Him, while He also revealed Himself through certain names. There is one name for the Lord that is used only once in the whole of Scripture, yet it echoes across every page. In Genesis 16, Hagar, the servant of Abram and Sarai is pregnant, and even though it was Sarai's idea that Abram make her pregnant, Sarai struggled to cope with the reality now before her. So she mistreated Hagar and as a result Hagar fled into the wilderness. But while she was there, the Lord met with her and saved her. Through that experience Hagar named the Lord, *El Roi* – the God who sees me.[5] Hagar wasn't just declaring that God sees, but by implication, *He saw her* and then acted on her behalf, thus saving and defending her. This was not passive sight, without pity or compassion, but rather this was seeing expressed in action – the eyes of the Lord that do!

As Jesus looked on the woman it was as if *El Roi* gazed upon her. Like Hagar she was an outcast, judged and mistreated, a woman despised and marginalised, and yet, His eyes were on her and He could truly see her. Before the storm of opposition could reach it's destructive crescendo, Jesus turned around and looked at her ... and at that moment, no one was going to harm her or hurt her.

Whether people see your extravagance for the Lord or even understand it, there is *One* who looks and sees you. So often in our journey to live extravagantly we are discouraged by the lack of appreciation of others, or the disingenuous words of friends. We may feel that all our efforts are in vain, that our service is unappreciated, our giving unnoticed and our gifts unnecessary. Yet, there is *One* who sees, *One* who takes note of every act of extravagance and every decision to do the right thing for Him, even though it may not be *seen* by the world around us. I love how the writer to the Hebrews puts it, when speaking to a community of believers who were feeling that their decision to follow Jesus was not being seen and they were suffering for it:

"God is not unjust; He will not forget your work and the love you have shown Him as you have helped His people and continue to help them." (Hebrews 6:10)

Did you notice that? Our love for *Him* is seen through our service to *His people*! The implication is that even if the people we are serving don't *see* what we've done for them in the name of the Lord, the Lord sees it and He will not forget it, or fail to reward it.

The world around us won't always *see* our extravagance for the Lord, but He sees it. *Simon* might miss it, but Jesus won't. *Simon* might criticise us, but Jesus will commend us. *Simon* might look with disgust, but the Lord will look with delight. Remember, we're not being extravagant for *Simon's* benefit, but for the Lord's, so we don't need or want or wait for *Simon's* appreciation when we know we have the affirmation of *El Roi*, the God who sees me. Our extravagance will always get His allegiance and catch His eye.

Her extravagance got His applause
"You did not ... but she..." (v44, 45 & 46)

Jesus highlights the passivity of Simon in contrast to the passionate extravagance of the woman. If it wasn't enough that Jesus turned to the woman and spoke to Simon while facing her, Rabbi Jesus makes a direct comparison between the actions of His host and those of the woman, putting her in a favourable light and in turn applauding her for her actions. The basic social etiquette not offered by Simon was exposed dramatically by the appalling extravagance of the woman when set side by side. The rhythm of the NIV portrays this beautifully, "you did not ... but she..."

Remember, as Jesus spoke these words He was looking directly at the woman. His goal was not to embarrass His host, He could have done that without referring to her, but rather His words are an acknowledgment and applause for what she has done. Note the detail of His words as He described her actions. Let me remind you that while she had served Him, He seemed unmoved and impassive, yet it is clear from His words to her and about her, that He missed nothing of what she did, as is highlighted in the detail of His applause.

"...but she wet my feet with her tears..."
The word used here in verse 44 for wet is exactly the same as that used to describe her actions in verse 38, emphasising the fact that her tears "rained" onto Him.

"...and wiped them with her hair..."
The phrasing of this statement echoes the dramatic moment when the woman unbound her hair and used it to towel His feet dry. Jesus does not skip over this awkward moment but rather celebrates it.

"...has not stopped kissing my feet..."
Not only does Jesus contrast the single kiss He might have expected from Simon as He entered his house, but He reemphasises the continuous nature of the woman's kissing, captured in verse 38 and now amplified by Jesus' own words.

Jesus noted that the woman hadn't just kissed Him, but she had kissed Him passionately and continuously.

"...she has poured perfume on my feet..."
Finally, Jesus did not miss the fact that the woman had poured or smeared, all of her perfume on Him. The tense of His words suggest that she had finished and that the contents of her bottle were now gone.

Why did Jesus do this, why does He replay the actions of the woman? There's no doubt that there's a "compare and contrast" moment happening here and that Jesus, by highlighting her, challenges Simon. But I'm certain Jesus' goal was not to embarrass His host any further. Rather, the replay is for the woman's sake. As Jesus played back the events, He got the details absolutely correct, both in order and action, showing that He was not only paying attention, but that her actions had impacted Him deeply and that the details were noted. The specific nature of His words represented high praise for the woman indeed. She was not offered a generic thank you, but rather every detail was appreciated and every nuance noted. *Jesus noticed everything and missed nothing!*

My eldest daughter Elaina got married in the summer of 2015 and it was one of the most amazing days of my life. Having walked her down the isle (trying to not cry ... I am Irish after all) and giving her away, I have a new found empathy for dads at wedding rehearsals. It's not as easy as it looks! Perhaps it was because it was my firstborn getting married, but I noticed the detail more. Elaina and Dan had gone to enormous energy on little but profound details. They had beautiful touches that might be missed by the general public but that carried weight for family – little touches that, if observed, spoke of a bigger picture and a deeper meaning. Because Elaina had invested so much into the details, she was thrilled when people noticed and understood them. Saturated with meaning, applause for the detail was high praise indeed. If anyone missed the detail I'm sure they still had an enjoyable day, but for me, it was this that made the day even more spectacular and memorable.

When heaven applauds extravagance it is always with the detail in mind. *The Lord notices everything and misses nothing.* He doesn't just feel tears, He sees rain. He knows the number of hairs used to towel His feet. Every kiss is counted and enjoyed and the cost of the perfume is weighed and understood. Just as He is the God of detail, so He delights in the detail of our offering, our worship and our sacrifice. He noticed that Abel brought the best of the best of his flock and that the woman put "two very small copper" coins into the offering plate of the temple.[6]

Extravagance will always find its reward sooner or later. He not only sees, He sees the detail, and nothing given in His name or for His glory is missed … nothing! Even when *we* forget the detail, the Lord does not and when we've forgotten the cost, He has everything on account. Sometimes we get the reward here and now and there's an immediate acknowledgment and applause. Then sometimes – if I'm honest, many times – details are missed, moments pass and the applause we felt we should have had doesn't come. It's at those times we remember the *audience of One*, that even if our spouse, our pastor, our friend or our church misses it … He hasn't, He has caught the moment, recorded it forever, and one day the details of our extravagance will be applauded.

John puts it this way, speaking of Jesus:

"Behold I am coming soon! My reward is with Me, and I will give to everyone according to what he has done. I am the Alpha and the Omega, the First and the Last, the Beginning and the End." (Revelation 22:12)

Jesus describes Himself in detail, which gives us confidence that He pays attention to detail. He assures us that because He is the "beginning and the end", He's got the detail in hand and that everything has been noticed and nothing has been missed. He sees, and has seen, the detail and that fact alone should encourage us to continue to live extravagantly for Him. One day (maybe today), but one day, He'll applaud the detail.

Our extravagance will always attract His applause ... He's in the detail!

Her extravagance got His approval

"Your faith has saved you; go in peace." (v50)

From a biblical record, we don't know for sure what happened to the woman after this story, but we do know one thing for certain: when she left that night, she left with the approval of Jesus ringing in her ears. Not only had He transformed her life, as evidenced in her extravagance that night, but He had defended and applauded her in a way, I venture to suggest, no man had ever done before. It is interesting that the phrase could literally read, "Go into peace." It may be worth noting that the rabbis held that "Go in peace" was proper in bidding farewell to the dead, but to the living one should say, "Go into peace".[7] She wasn't dead – she was alive! Jesus was not only approving of her actions, but of her future, commending her to it and encouraging her to take the opportunity for life now afforded to her.

To approve carries with it the idea of *officially agreeing* with something and/or to *accept something as satisfactory.* In this most public of moments and with this final statement to the woman, Jesus is certainly doing both. As we've already established, the actions of the woman are the sign that she had already encountered Jesus and came that night forgiven, and that her extravagance is the moment she came out as a follower of Jesus. So now Jesus reciprocates her public extravagance with public endorsement, speaking words to her that in truth were already a reality within her. But these words are now spoken in front of a gathered audience. She knew, now they know! Jesus put His approval on the woman so that no one would be in any doubt as to what had happened to her and why she did what she did.

We all need a sense of approval, no matter who we are. As followers of Jesus, our primary approval comes from our identity not our actions. It is in understanding who we are and that we are unconditionally loved as children of God, which will provide the greatest and most liberating reason for our approval. However, from that identity, we can also find an approval from the Lord in the things we do for Him. He loves us whether we do those things or not, but when we learn to live in a way that pleases Him, we experience the official agreement of heaven and the acceptance that something is good.

I love my three children passionately, and nothing they do will ever change that. They are loved primarily because of who they are, not because of any achievement, thus they are approved as they are. However, I love it and am pleasured when they do things I like or want without me asking them for it. When that happens, they aren't more loved, but they experience a different type of approval, one that has moved beyond their identity and into their behaviour. This is an approval that further empowers their actions, letting them know that what they've done is appreciated and that to continue to live this way would bring me great pleasure.

Paul encourages the church at Ephesus:

"...find out what pleases the Lord." (Ephesians 5:10)

The word "pleases" is *euárestos* and is made up of two words namely, "well" and "to please". Paul wants us to *well please* the Lord – to intentionally find out what He likes and then do it. This is not random or haphazard, this is the result of catching His heart, understanding His ways, hearing His word and then making a decision to do the sort of things He actually likes.

David declares,

"Blessed is the man who fears the Lord, who finds great delight in His commands." (Psalm 112:1)

When we delight חָפֵץ (*chafetz*), when we are mindful, attentive, intentional and take pleasure in the Lord's commands, or what He wants, then He blesses us, approves of our actions and demonstrates His approval by doing for us something only He can do.

That night, the woman came as one already approved, but somehow she understood what would please Him, and so she gave to Him her extravagant offering. We live as children of God, already approved in and by His love, but He looks for a man or woman who will catch His heart, understand what He wants and generously and extravagantly give it to Him. When He finds such an offering, He is not slow in demonstrating His approval.

The extravagance of the woman undoubtedly irritated Simon, but as we have seen, it more than impressed Jesus. Her actions that night got His attention, allegiance, applause and approval and although it was not her intention to do so, her extravagance exposed the passionless void of those around her. It seems that the woman, though relatively new to the idea of following Jesus, understood one of the greatest principles of followership: live for the audience of *One!*

Endnotes

1. 1 Peter 5:5
2. Deuteronomy 31:17-18 (these are the Lord's words to Moses) & Job 13:24 (this is how Job interpreted his trouble)
3. Genesis 4:1-5
4. Luke 21:1-4
5. Genesis 16:1-16
6. See footnote 3 & 4
7. Morris, p149.

Chapter 10 – Extravagance is Not For Everyone

On the surface of it, the title of this chapter seems to be a contradiction to the trajectory of the message within this book, and in a sense it is. Theoretically, anyone can be extravagant and it's my hope that through this book, readers will be encouraged into a lifestyle of genuine extravagance towards the Lord. However, just as in our story, there are those who seem to hold back from *"passing the bounds of reason, being wild, absurd, flamboyant, abundant or even wasteful"*, and there are others who don't seem to have any difficulty crossing the lines and showing the object of their passion, just how they feel! As in our story, so in life – it would be too simplistic to label Simon as bad and the woman as good, or to suggest that Simon didn't love God and the woman did. Though, on the one hand, extravagance is for everyone, and the Lord would call each of us to it, I have discovered that it's not for everyone, and that for one reason or another some people who claim to be followers of Jesus, demonstrate from their attitudes and actions a less than generous lifestyle. It was Dietrich Bonhoeffer who said, "Your life as a Christian should make non-believers question their disbelief in God." Yet sometimes, if we're honest, the life of some Christians might cause us to question *their* belief in God. Surely, if the Lord of the universe lives within us the outcome would automatically be a life of extravagance, right?

Over the years I've heard (and made) excuses as to why people can't or won't be extravagant. Here are my top four.

Excuse #1: It's not my personality type

"I'm not like that" can feel and sound like an appropriate excuse when confronted with the over-the-top approach of the woman. "She's clearly one of those extroverts and likes that sort of stuff, but that's not me...". I totally get the reasoning, for I am a reluctant extrovert and, over the years, I've had to coach and encourage my introversion in a Pentecostal context that loves extroverts and largely browbeats introverts. I've had to manage deep levels of discomfort in settings where I was expected to behave a certain way, even though I wasn't ready or persuaded to do so. I'm more than happy for others to get on with it, whatever it is (provided it's moral and legal), but I'm always uneasy when I'm being "forced" to be like them to prove my love for Jesus, and judged unfairly when I'm not.

If you've ever had the experience of a large sporting event or concert, personality excuses tend to fade away. I've watched football with thousands of people of all personality types, yet I've heard them sing (sometimes not very well) at the top of their voices, screaming, shouting and chanting for their team on the pitch. For a few moments, their focus is taken off themselves and projected onto their team, thus they forget about themselves and enter into what could only be described as an extravagant form of worship, albeit not Jesus centred! No one uses their personality type as an excuse at a sporting event, so why use it in the Church or in the context of serving Jesus?

There's no denying our personality, in fact, the Lord celebrates it, but we must not allow it to become a shallow excuse not to obey a glorious call. In truth, we've no idea of the personality type of the woman, all we know is that she served so extravagantly that we're still talking about her 2000 years later. That evening her eyes were so fixed on Him that she stopped thinking about herself, and the rest, as they say, is history. Maybe, if we shifted our focus off ourselves and placed it onto Him, it would transform our behaviour without changing our personality!

Excuse #2: My story isn't that exciting

My grandfather was radically converted in the mid 1950s. Before then he'd lived a pretty extreme life, having returned from World War II in 1945 after fighting for almost five years in Burma. My grandfather loved to drink, smoke, gamble and fight, until the night he met Jesus and his life changed forever. I used to love to hear his story, of what he was and what he became. As a boy who became a follower of Jesus aged eight, my life, my story seemed totally boring by comparison. However, my grandfather reminded me many times that my story was just as remarkable as his. Though Jesus had saved him from a life of extravagant sin, he always celebrated the fact that the Lord had kept me from such a life and saved me from it in more ways than one.

On one level my story isn't that exciting. I'm not likely to be picked for a tour featuring "amazing stories and testimonies", and so the danger is for me to think of my story as less important, less valuable and less radical. But the story we've been working through together reminds us that debt is debt and sin is sin, and if one can't pay then it doesn't matter what the amount is, we're stuffed!

The truth is, my unpayable debt (which seems a lot smaller than my grandfather's) has been cancelled and in its place, Jesus has put wealth beyond my wildest dreams. Whether saved at eight or eighty, if we can grasp this simple but profound truth, it has the power to change how we look at everything. I've now come to the conclusion that my story *is* exciting. I was a sinner and now I'm a saint. I was in the debt of sin and now my debt has been cancelled and credit put into my account. I was lost but now I'm found. I was an enemy of God but now I'm a citizen in His kingdom. I was a slave but now I'm a son. I was dead but now I'm alive. I was far off but now I am brought near! When I recall this, it seems my story is as exciting as anyone's, so there's no excuse then not to be extravagant.

Excuse #3: I don't have much to offer

I once heard a preacher say that this woman's gift was a one-off and Jesus wouldn't expect him to give such an offering. In one sense I totally agree, although to say it was a one-off, isn't quite true if we regard the anointing in Matthew, Mark and John as a different event. I don't think Jesus is requiring me to do exactly what the woman did or even necessarily be preoccupied with matching the financial extravagance of her offering. However, I am convinced that the spirit and attitude displayed by the woman is something I can connect to and be inspired by. What I must not do is compare what I have, or what I can give to what the woman did. After all, the gift she gave that night could never be repeated in that way again by her, because of the uniqueness of the offering. If we live in the world of comparison, we'll never give anything, and if we do, we'll give it with the wrong attitude and for the wrong reasons, which means it can never be extravagant. We are not called to copy the woman, but I do believe we're being asked to demonstrate the same heart, however it might be practically displayed. Extravagance can and will look like a million things, but an extravagant attitude looks and sounds the same no matter what gift is offered.

When we focus on what we're giving, we're already off target. Rather we're called to fix our eyes on the One we're giving it to and why we want Him to have it. When this happens, the size of the gift is eclipsed by the spirit with which it is given – and that's the perfume that pleases the Lord.

Excuse #4: The Lord knows I love Him

During my wedding reception, the floor was opened and any of our guests were invited to give a speech (a slightly unusual and risky thing to do, but we got away with it). I remember one older gentleman standing to offer his congratulations and advice to us. He looked at me and said these words:

'Young man, tell your wife you love her every day!'

These are the sort of words one would expect to hear on a wedding day, but somehow they struck into my heart, and I have endeavoured to follow his advice. Every day I attempt to tell my incredible wife Dawn that I love her, whether that be in words or deeds. But it would be so easy to fall back into the complacency of "she knows I love her, therefore I don't need to keep telling her". Let's not worry about presents for birthdays, anniversaries and Christmas … let's just bask in the glory of our unspoken love for each other. You and I know that would be a recipe for disaster and no matter how strong we think our marriages and relationships are, we must never accept the lie that love can or should remain unspoken or undemonstrated.

Jesus knew Peter loved Him, but He still asked him the question three times and each time made a request that would in turn demonstrate Peter's love for and to Him.[1] Even though the Lord knows all things, including the motivations of our hearts, He still asks for "evidence" of love – a sign that, in fact, He is at the centre of everything. He asks for a cut of our wealth, for the central place in our hearts and for a relentless commitment to His agenda to save the world. When speaking to His own disciples, Jesus put it so simply:

"If you love Me, you will obey what I command." (John 14:15)

The Lord does know you love Him, but that's not a "get out of being extravagant" card. Rather, it should really be the catalyst in our hearts to show Him by our words and actions what He already knows. If you love Him, show Him!

Though there may be some validity to these excuses, our story shows us a deeper more uncomfortable truth that takes us beyond the superficiality of such meagerness. Our four excuses hide a deeper reality that affords us little shelter when its spotlight is shone into our hearts. If we learn anything from the extravagance of the woman and the reaction of Simon it's that *every act of faith flows from a revelation of truth!* Extravagance is an action of faith and faith is the offspring of revelation. The woman served because she saw something, whereas Simon remained frozen in apathy because he just did not see what she saw.

During the writing of this book, our two Dachshunds, Pepperoni and Salami, got together and made six beautiful puppies (an experience that has been more nerve-wracking for me than having three children!). Of course, pictures of our gorgeous grand-puppies started to appear across social media in regular *pupdates*. One picture features my wife Dawn holding one of the pups to Pepperoni so he could sniff his offspring for the first time. It was a lovely shot. Of the comments left one read, "It's time to get him (Pepperoni) 'done' then...", while another read, "Oh wow, just so sweet, powerful pic :)". Isn't it amazing how two people can see the same picture and yet articulate very different responses? Of course, the comments really say more about them than what they are seeing. Isn't this so true of us all. Our actions and words are a reflection of what we see and how we see it, whether that is my *pupdate* or Jesus.

Though we can use our excuses to legitimise our lack of extravagance, the truth is our excuses are an attempt to distract our world from the reality of our hearts. The truth is we don't serve because we don't see. If Simon had seen what she saw he would have done what she did – maybe not in the same way precisely, but appropriate to his personality and context. Remember, *every act of faith flows form a revelation of truth* and faith is the offspring of revelation! We behave because we believe and we serve because we see!

So regardless of our personality type, our story, the size of our gift or the belief that the Lord knows we love Him, extravagance can and will flow from our lives when our eyes are opened to three life-transforming truths.

We see who He is

I never really gave giraffe's much of a thought until I saw one in the wilds of Africa and now I think they're fab. While on a ministry trip, I was given the opportunity to go on safari during some down time and I grabbed it. Feeling adventurous I even opted for the horseback tour, even though I can't ride a horse … I'm not quite sure what I was thinking. While we were out on the trail, our guide would point out various animals and it was very exciting. However, at one point on the tour he stopped his horse (and miraculously mine stopped too) and pointed to a small bunch of trees. I obviously followed his finger and squinted into the sun. After a while, feeling a little awkward, I asked, "What am I looking at?" thinking trees weren't part of the tour. He answered, "The bull giraffe, right there among the trees!" I looked again and saw nothing against the burnt orange horizon, so I looked back at him. Without saying a word his facial expression said it all, so I tried again. Then suddenly there was the slightest movement and there he was, where he had been all the time, *hidden* in the trees. Amazingly, once my eyes got him I wondered how on earth I had missed something so big and obvious, but I did! In fact, I would have put money on it (good job I'm not a betting man) that no giraffe was there – yet he was there all the time.

John declared,

"He was in the world, and though the world was made through Him, the world did not recognise Him. He came to that which was His own, but His own did not receive Him." (John 1:10-11)

It's hard to receive what we cannot see – and if we can't see it, we can't see it!

Extravagance is a sign that we see Him. When we see Him, we see something of the glory of God, we see grace and truth rolled together in one mind-blowing incarnational moment and we see Someone who has the power to transform our lives. When we see Him, everything changes and nothing can stay the same. When we can't see Him, everything stays the same and nothing changes!

Thomas missed the resurrected Lord when He appeared to the group, and as one might expect, he refused to be comforted or motivated by *their revelation*; he wanted his own.

"Unless I see the nail marks in His hands ... I will not believe."

Jesus appeared to him and Thomas made one of the greatest confessions in the New Testament:

"My Lord and my God."

This is the first time in the New Testament record that this confession was used in this form and, for a Jewish boy, the combination of God and Lord, all directed at Jesus was revolutionary indeed. Note too the personal nature of the confession, *"My* Lord ... *my* God." Thomas wasn't passing on what others had seen, rather, he was now confessing what he saw! When he saw Jesus, everything changed.[2]

Is it possible to see Him and remain small and stingy? Is it possible to truly see Him and an extravagant lifestyle not ensue? The woman saw Him and expensive perfume filled the room. Simon missed Him and awkward excuses filled his heart!

We see what He has done

Gladys seemed ancient when I first met her. I was thirty years old and about to step into my second church and Gladys was, well, much, much older. She was also paralysed down one side of her upper body, which meant she only had the use of one arm. I found out later that she never married because she chose to look after both her aged parents until they died, thus sacrificing certain freedoms and opportunities in her own life. Gladys seemed like just another old lady until I got to know her. I found out she had a "wicked" sense of humour and a very extravagant heart. With no family to speak of, Gladys was determined to enrich her world in whatever way she could with the gifts God had given her – and that she did. One remarkable time (and there were many others), I saw Gladys give a gift to a missionary couple visiting our church. Moved by the amazing work they were doing with children, Gladys gave them some money towards building and supporting their work. So what, I hear you say, lots of people do that. True, but Gladys, who is now in heaven, gave them £7,000 cash! Apart from her, only two people knew she was going to do that, myself and another pastor who watched out for her. I watched her as she reached out to give the gift with her one good arm, and squeeze the wad of notes into the shocked missionary's hand. As Gladys walked out that evening, most people saw an aging lady with a bit of stoop and a paralysed arm … but I saw a giant, an extravagantly generous saint of God who demonstrated her love for Him by blessing others and changing their world. My knowledge of her changed how I viewed her and the Lord enjoyed the perfume coming from her gift.

In our story, it is fascinating that the woman turns up because Jesus has already forgiven her of her sin, a fact we covered in great detail in a previous chapter, yet, when Simon's guests eventually speak up, that is the one thing they question:

"Who is this who even forgives sins?" (Luke 7:49)

What they were questioning she already knew and had experienced. She understood what He had done for her and her response was extravagance. However, they were certain He could not do what He claimed He did and therefore their response was skepticism and doubt.

An understanding and acceptance of what He has done for us should catalyse our extravagance for Him. When describing what Jesus has done, Paul's summary to the Philippian church sums it up gloriously:

"Who, being in very nature God, did not consider equality with God something to be grasped, but made Himself nothing, taking the very nature of a servant, being made in human likeness. And being found in appearance as a man, He humbled Himself and became obedient to death – even death on a cross." (Philippians 2:5-8)

Is it then any wonder Paul, after describing the goodness of the Lord in our savlation could say:

"Therefore I urge you, brothers, in view of God's mercy, to offer your bodies as living sacrifices, holy and pleasing to God – this is your spiritual act of worship." (Romans 12:1)

When we see what He has done, there's always a "therefore". We can't just leave it there, hanging as a fact to be studied. When we see what He has done it demands a "therefore". It is interesting, as in Romans, where Paul's "therefore" follows eleven chapters of glorious grace which demands an extravagant response, that similarly in Philippians "therefore" heralds the opportunity for extravagance. In Romans, Paul calls us to be extravagant in offering our bodies, but in Philippians, Paul declares that the Father was extravagant when he concludes,

"Therefore God exalted Him to the highest place and gave Him a name that is above every name..." (Philippians 2:9-11)

Having seen and understood what Jesus did, the Father

responds with extravagance! Having seen and understood what Jesus did, Paul urges us to do the same by giving Him the most precious commodity we own ... our lives.

When we see what He has done for us, extravagance is the only option available!

We see how much we've got

In 2003, American antique experts launched a campaign to encourage people to check their garages, basements and attics for anything that might look like an antique. They received a call from a resident of Boston, Massachusetts, who had found a painting in her attic and had no idea if it had any worth. Auctioneer John McInnis was dispatched to take a look. Climbing into the attic he saw a landscape painting depicting the North Shore of New England, USA, by a 19th Century painter called Martin Johnson Heade. Heade's works had been virtually uncelebrated during his lifetime, but during the 1940s they experienced a renaissance and had slowly gained acceptance and status. As John McInnis examined the 12 x 26 inch unnamed piece (now entitled *River Scene*), as it leaned against the attic rafter, he noticed it was still in its original gilded frame and became quite excited. Apparently, the painting had been in the attic for 60 years ... unnoticed and untouched! McInnis persuaded the owner to offer it up for auction and on 7th December 2003, the painting sold for $1,006,250![3]

#Boom!!!

Previously, another one of his paintings, *Gold Velvet Cloth*, had been "covering up a hole in a wall" in Indiana, and in 1999 was sold to the Museum of Fine Arts in Houston for $1,250,000! Okay, slowly put the book down, go now and check your attic for any works of art and remember me when you sell it for millions! Wow, what a thought that a work of art, worth a small fortune was sitting in the attic for all those years. A life-changing sum of money was gathering dust in the guise of what looked like a worthless painting.

For years I have had the privilege of serving the Church of Jesus and in that time I've seen this reality over and over again, where wonderful followers of Jesus have no idea what they've already got. I hear a lot of people asking the Lord for more, but how refreshing it is when I meet someone who has a true sense of who they are and what they've got in Jesus, and are content to live in and from that position of staggering wealth. Paul put it magnificently when he wrote to the Ephesian church:

"Praise be to the God and Father of our Lord Jesus Christ, who has blessed us in the heavenly realms with every spiritual blessing in Christ." (Ephesians 1:3)

To the Corinthians, speaking of Jesus he concludes, "Thanks be to God for His indescribable gift" (2 Corinthians 9:15).

Paul got it and that's why he gave of himself so relentlessly and extravagantly throughout his life. He understood what he was and where he had come from, and he had a profound realisation of what he had in Christ. Though the chief of sinners, Paul walked in the revelation that he had been entrusted with the glorious Gospel, so it's no wonder he exclaimed from a prison cell:

"For me to live is Christ and to die is gain." (Philippians 1:21)

There may not be a Heade in the attic, but there is a Saviour within your heart. What might change if we realised what we actually have right now? If we truly believed that we have received everything in Christ, that He is God's indescribable gift, that life is Christ and death is gain? Surely then our only response would be extravagance to Him, giving Him what He asks for and doing it with enthusiasm and passion.

Extravagance is not for everybody because not everyone will see who He is, not everyone will see what He has done and not everyone will see how much they've got. Extravagance is an action of faith and a sign that we see beyond ourselves to something, Someone greater than us. Every act of faith flows from a revelation of truth because faith is the offspring of revelation. Though all eyes were on the woman that night, her eyes were on Him and that's why she did what she did. In Simon's home she *"passed the bounds of reason, was wild, absurd, flamboyant, abundant and even wasteful"*, because she wasn't looking at the offering, rather she was consumed by the Saviour. When He is our vision, what excuse is there not to be extravagant?

Endnotes
1. John 21:15-19
2. John 20:24-29
3. Featured on the PBS program Find and now hands in the Fogg Art Museum in Cambridge Massachusetts.

Chapter 11 – Actions Speak Louder Than Words

One of the most remarkable facts about our story is that the woman does not speak. Throughout the fourteen verses Dr Luke spoke, Jesus spoke, Simon spoke and even Simon's guests spoke, but she, the woman at the epicentre of the controversy, said nothing. There is no attempt on her part to explain herself to Jesus or defend herself to Simon. Rather, she let her actions do the talking whilst leaving the words to others. That night there was no need for words, because her actions said it all. The phrase, "actions speak louder than words" isn't found in the Bible, but the spirit of these words is captured throughout the Scriptures framed in a theology that teaches *doing is believing*. Of all the people in the room that evening, she was by far the least qualified to argue theology and the nuances of the sacred text, but her actions preached a message so loud that no one in the room was able to ignore it.

Words, of course, are important as Dr Luke's record and hopefully this book you are reading testify. We only have the story of the woman anointing Jesus because someone wrote it down and their words were preserved beyond the fading memories of 1st Century believers. I believe in words – our faith is built on words and without words of truth we would have no substance from which to frame our lives. So in exploring the actions of the woman, I am not minimising the importance of words, rather I am highlighting through her experience the fact that actions can speak as loudly as words, and sometimes louder. She was silent, yet she spoke!

Why then can actions speak louder than words? Through the example of the woman, I want to draw out four possibilities.

Actions declare what we really believe

The woman could have sent Jesus a note thanking Him for changing her life and expressing to Him her undying love. She could have gone privately to synagogue and said a prayer or visited the Temple in Jerusalem and given a sacrifice, all of which would have been perfectly acceptable. However, she chose to express her belief that evening in a particularly extravagant way, demonstrating what she thought of Jesus and how deeply she believed what she believed. The tears, unbound hair, kisses and expensive perfumed nard, were all signposts to the faith she now cherished. The woman could simply have said verbally, "I am a follower," but instead, she spoke the same truth through her actions because for her, *doing was believing.*

I have met a lot of people over the years who believe they believe a lot of things. The problem with belief that remains locked in our head is that it is easy to believe we really believe, without what we believe ever being put to the test! We all believe things about ourselves which, when put to the test, are just not true. For example, most people will think of themselves as being fairly generous with others, yet a quick glance at our bank statement might reveal that most of our money, one way or the other, goes on us. I regard myself as pretty tolerant and patient, yet recently I was on a flight where a rather large man beside me elbowed himself into my space and, on top of that, he was smelly. I didn't enjoy the flight very much and as we landed I concluded I wasn't even a Christian! Had you asked me in my neat, comfortable, lovely smelling office if I was patient, I would have (with great humility, of course) said that I was ... but the plane flight showed me otherwise!

It's relatively easy to say, "I believe in Jesus" or "I love the Church" or "I want to see the world saved" and they are all good things to say. But these words mean absolutely nothing unless they find some expression in our actions. Too many see theology as an academic extra, a sort of thinking-room part of our lives where we can hold certain ideas without being challenged to put them into practice. But this is an alien idea in the Scriptures, where we are challenged with the truth that *doing is believing* – not simply as evidence of our belief, but as belief itself.

When trying to help the people, and at the same time challenging the scholars of His day, Jesus said these words:

> "The teachers of the law and the Pharisees sit in Moses' seat. So you must be careful to do everything they tell you. But do not do what they do, for they do not practice what they preach." (Matthew 23:2-3)

We get our phrase "practice what you preach" from these verses and, at the heart of them, they represent two powerful ideas when it comes to belief.

Authenticity
When Jesus told the people to listen but not look, this would

have felt like a deep insult to the religious community. Jesus commended their theology, but exposed the incongruence between what they said they believed and how they behaved (or didn't behave) as belief. If the two things don't come together, though the words are good and have the power in themselves to bring life, the person delivering them is to be ignored as an example of those words. Authenticity points to the genuineness of something, so when Jesus marks the religious as inauthentic, He is in fact not just questioning their behaviour, but their belief.

John puts it another way when echoing Jesus:

"Dear children, let us not love with words or speech but with actions and in truth." (1 John 3:18)

The implication of truth in this context is of something being real and genuine, rather than having an appearance of being so. Thus, for John our actions are true, not only an expression of truth. If the world is to truly understand love as the Christian community frames it, then that belief must move beyond words into deeds. John argues that if we truly believe in this love, it will express itself in action.

Authority

Had the woman turned up that night and announced to everyone, "My life has been changed, I'm a follower of Jesus," many in the room might have taken her on and challenged her position. However, as uncomfortable as her extravagant actions were, they were undeniable as a sign that something dramatic had happened to her. Her actions added authority to the claim that Jesus made on her behalf: "...her many sins have been forgiven...". She was acting like a woman who had been set free, whose death sentence had been commuted.

This is echoed in the story of Zacchaeus, a chief tax collector who was called down out of a tree so that Jesus might have dinner with him at his house! As a result of that encounter Zacchaeus did something and made a promise:

"Look, Lord! Here and now I give half of my possessions to the poor, and if I have cheated anybody out of anything, I will pay back four times the amount."

Note the reaction of Jesus:

"Today salvation has come to this house..."[1]

The announcement of salvation was made on the evidence of Zacchaeus' action. Salvation wasn't proclaimed over him because of what he believed, because he "raised his hand" or "filled in a decision card". Rather, salvation was announced on the evidence of a changed life, demonstrated by actions of restitution and restoration. Salvation was announced on the basis of what he did.

Like John, James echoes the words and teaching of Jesus when he concludes:

"...faith by itself, if it is not accompanied by action, is dead." (James 2:17)

Anyone can say they believe, but the evidence of belief is in the actions it produces. If there's no fruit, there's no root! That's why actions speak louder than words, because anyone can say something, but doing is different; it's a step beyond, moving us from theory to practice and from ideal to reality. Too many hide behind words of faith, when Jesus is looking for the extravagant actions of faith. The woman doesn't say a word and yet we hear her say, *doing is believing*.

Actions put our money where our mouth is
We've already looked at the potential expense of this gift in a

previous chapter, so I'm not proposing to go over old ground on this, other than to say … it was expensive! The events of that night cost this woman dearly and yet she was prepared to pay it and do so without hesitation. The clear intentionality of her action meant she had weighed the cost and still decided to do it. Jesus was worth her offering and He was worthy of any cost she now incurred. In putting her money where her mouth was, she let everyone know what she truly believed.

Extravagance will always cost, especially when it is associated with something or someone we passionately believe in. In fact, it's when something starts to cost that we find out how much we really believe in it. We like the idea of taking up our cross occasionally, but we're not so keen on the idea of taking it up daily! We like the idea of giving what's in our heart to give, but we don't like it when someone puts figures like 10%, 20% or 30% in our face. We like the idea of calling our local church home, but are less taken with the fact that we have to contribute to actually make it home.

Everything of value costs, and what we claim to believe in is no different. If I say I believe in my marriage, it will cost. Family costs, building a good business costs and being a follower of Jesus costs. The idea that we can believe without contributing and without it demanding something of our behaviour, time or wealth is an alien concept in the Bible. Yet so many want the benefits of extravagant grace while living a stingy, tight-fisted lifestyle.

What would your behaviour to the Lord say about your belief in Him?

Is it a "just enough" faith or a "He understands that I don't do extravagance" faith or maybe "He gets what is left-over" faith? What we do and how we do it communicates to the world around us what we actually believe. We can try to deflect and defend, but in a world where *doing is believing*, there's nowhere to hide. Solomon put it this way:

"Like clouds and wind without rain is one who boasts of gifts never given." (Proverbs 25:14)

When it comes to belief, this is a trap many fall into. We promise much but never really deliver, we swear allegiance, but rarely show up and with our words we believe, but our behaviour asks the question, *do we?*

That night, everyone knew what the woman believed without her saying a word. By putting her money where her mouth was and placing a price tag on her belief, she demonstrated the depth of her conviction and extent of her passion. When actions cost, they always speak louder than words!

Actions get our attention

Had the woman turned up with a finely tuned script to read to Simon and his esteemed guests, I'm not sure she would have made it through the first paragraph. The likelihood is that the brains in the room would have taken her words apart and made her look small and inadequate. Failing that, someone would have helped her find the exit! This was, after all, a room of words. Simon (who had not acted well towards Jesus), had designed the night so that a war of words could be fought and hopefully he and his friends would be the victors. This was a night when the finer points of the Law might be discussed and the Galilean Rabbi challenged on some of His more interesting ideas.

So it is striking that in a room of words it was an action that stopped everyone in their tracks and changed the agenda of the evening. Any words spoken by a sinful woman that night would have been lost in the noise and brilliance of the other words in the room, but her appalling behaviour … no one expected that! It was her actions that got the attention of the room, and they spoke louder than any of her words could have!

In 1913 Emily Davidson threw herself in front of the King's horse during the Epsom Derby, sustaining injuries that led to her death four days later. As a women's suffrage activist she had been imprisoned nine times and even suffered the horror of being force-fed while on hunger strike. Her actions catapulted the issue of women's rights into the forefront of society. It got people's attention!

Ghandi said, "We need to be the change we wish to see in the world." These are great words, but it was action that started to galvanise his pre-independent nation of India. In 1930 he led thousands across India in what became known as the *Salt March*, in opposition to a salt tax imposed on imported salt by the British. The tax impacted every Indian and his twenty-four day march captured their imagination.

In 1968 in Mexico, Tommie Smith won the Olympic gold medal in the men's 200m for USA. However, it was when he received his medal along with fellow American bronze medalist John Carlos that controversy broke out. As their national anthem was played, both men raised a clenched, gloved fist in the air, as a political gesture for their support of the civil and human rights movement for black people in America. He said, "If I win I am an American, not a black American. But if I did something bad they would say I am a Negro. We are black and we are proud of being black. Black America will understand what we did tonight." There were lots of words being spoken in America and around the world at that time on the issues of civil and human rights, but that night, two men on a podium got the world's attention.[2]

I could, of course, go on and on with examples of actions getting the attention of the world of words. The fact is, words can be ignored and countered with other words and a war of words can be fought. But every now and again, even on a global stage, our eyes have been arrested by the actions of an individual or group of people that causes us to stop, shut up and look!

Words are easier to ignore than actions. Though we're bombarded with more words than ever through social media, email and texting, the power to deflect, ignore or even delete these words has also grown. I'm better at ignoring certain words than I've ever been. Every day on social media I'm tempted to climb in, but by and large I behave. If someone sends me a text, it can wait until I'm ready. But if someone turns up at the door, that's a different scenario altogether. Their action has changed the way I might respond. I can, of course, hide in the kitchen and try to stop my sausage dogs from barking, or I can answer the door and address the issue. Their action has got my attention in a way that maybe their words would not have.

That's why faith is about action, not just words. As the Bible declares:

"For God so loved the world that He *spoke*...".

No of course not, it reads:

"For God so loved the world that He *gave*..."

God's giving was a result and an expression of what He believed about His world and us, but it was the giving that got the world's attention and ultimately changed the world's direction. We must remember that people hear with their eyes! They hear through what they see in the actions of those around them. So often they cannot hear us because of what they see in us, but other times they hear us because of what they see through us.

When the room is filled with the noise of words and clever arguments rule the day, we must not underestimate the power of belief-fuelled action. That can get the attention of the room by demonstrating generously and positively, as the woman did, what real faith looks like. Actions have the potential of getting our attention in a way that words cannot and that's why they can speak louder than words.

Actions create memories
It is interesting that in the similar story found in Matthew, Mark and John, Jesus makes a remarkable statement about Mary's actions:

"I tell you the truth, wherever the gospel is preached throughout the world, what she has done will also be told, in memory of her." (Mark 14:9)

Her outstanding action created a lasting memory and I'm sure that those present that day, the disciples included, would have talked in later years of the time Mary anointed Jesus.

Looking back on my childhood, most of the things I recall my parents saying to me are associated with things they did with me. For me, words fade unless they are committed to memory intentionally, whereas events, experiences and connections last more naturally. I can remember the fact that my dad used to take me out to a restaurant on Christmas Eve as a special treat. We'd go down into Belfast City Centre and get fish and chips ... sitting in! I can recall Christmas mornings, where the whole family would descend the stairs to the living room in the specific order of dad first, then mum, then Margaret my sister, Alex my brother and then me. Dad would always open the door of the living room, look in and say (every year), "Santa hasn't been!" before leading us in to see what presents we'd received. I remember holiday picnics on the way to the North Coast of Ireland, where even though it was a relatively short journey from Belfast to Portrush, my dad insisted on stopping, having some tea and fun before completing the journey. There are, of course, words associated with all these events, but I have no struggle remembering the events themselves.

My dad became a pastor much later in life, in fact in his late fifties. It was an honour for him to serve the church he had attended all his life and he was thrilled to be taking on the role. A special celebration service was organised for him in which he was inducted as the new pastor, but because the date clashed with something I was doing, I told my dad I could not come. What I didn't tell him was that I managed to move stuff around and as a family we organised my surprise appearance during the service. At a certain moment in the ceremony, I was brought out from the back of the church onto the stage to greet my father. His face and reaction were priceless and we had a wonderful time. For years to come, my dad referred to that night and that moment when I walked out and surprised him. Without watching the video, he struggled to recall everything I said, but he never, ever forgot what I did … and how it made him feel!

The *Learning Pyramid* holds fear and terror for anyone who loves verbal communication as a form of teaching and learning. Within the pyramid there are four passive areas of learning (where the student receives from someone), namely, lecturing, reading, audio-visual and demonstration. Research has shown that the retention rates within these four areas are as follows:

Lecture – 5% retention
Reading – 10% retention
Audio-visual – 20% retention
Demonstration – 30% retention

The pyramid also shows three active or participatory styles of teaching/learning and they are, group discussion, practise by doing and teaching others. Research has shown that the retention rates within these three areas are as follows:

Group discussion – 50% retention
Practice by doing – 75% retention
Teaching others – 90% retention[3]

Enough said I think! Though everything must be evaluated, you and I know intuitively that the more we participate in something, or see something demonstrated, potentially the more powerful that is in both communicating to us and helping us to remember what we saw and learned. Words alone (and I speak as a preacher) have the lowest form of retention, and yet so often we maintain this as the key medium of learning and communication.

I'm a passionate believer in words and the memorisation of important words, but I also recognise the power of an event, an experience and even of something *felt* in a learning moment. Actions create memories in a way that words do not. Someone once said to me, "Memories are the library of our imagination" and that is powerful idea, which if true means that actions can speak louder than words. Actions with words, of course, are a potent combination, and when both go together, a memory can be created that can fuel our imagination for years to come. When we think of the story of this woman, the event helps frame the words in a way that mean they can be remembered more easily. When we can visualise what she did and why she did it, it is easier to recall the life-changing words Jesus spoke during this event.

I don't know if Simon and his friends ever made a move towards Jesus or became His followers after that night, but I'm willing to believe they never forgot that night. It would be wonderful to think that days, weeks or years later, Simon reflected on the evening, recalled the appalling extravagance of the woman, remembered the painful exposition of Jesus, and maybe, just maybe, surrendered his life to the same truth he had so dramatically encountered in his home. If there is indeed a media library in heaven with a section entitled "What happened next", then I'll have a little look to see if there's anything labelled *Simon the Pharisee, his life after Luke 7...* I'm hoping so anyway!

Loved or loathed, the woman's extravagance, her behaviour that "*passed the bounds of reason ... wild, absurd, flamboyant, abundant and even wasteful*", caught the attention of everyone in the room. No one would ever forget what she did, and accompanied by the words of Jesus, why she did it. Though in Dr Luke's story, she's the only character that doesn't speak, her message is heard loud and clear and her "sermon" reached every heart. The woman reminds us that extravagance can never remain just an idea, or even be limited to words alone, no matter how eloquent. Rather, to be extravagant is to act, to do and to demonstrate! It is through our actions that our true beliefs are expressed and the greater the cost, the deeper the conviction. Anyone can talk, but not everyone does, and as far as the message of the Bible is concerned, *doing is believing*. If we don't do, we don't believe, and if we don't do extravagantly, we don't believe deeply! Twenty-one centuries later, we're still talking about the actions of a *prostitute* in the house of a religious man. Even with the challenges of cultural context she still captures our imagination and prods us for a response. In fourteen verses she doesn't say a word, yet she speaks to us with clarity and dignity.

What could you say today without opening your mouth?

What message could you deposit through an act of intentional extravagance to the Lord, His people and His world?

What memory could you create in someone's mind, which seeds the library of their imagination?

If she did it, we can do it. If she spoke through her actions, so can we. If, through her doing, she demonstrated her believing, then what's stopping you and I from showing the world that actions speak louder than words?

"But wisdom is proved right by all her children."

Endnotes

1. Luke 19:1-10
2. www.one.org
3. www.thepeakperformancecenter.com as one example of the learning pyramid

Chapter 12 – A New Normal

As we come to the end of this book and draw the curtain on the extravagance of the woman, it is my hope that our journey to the heart of extravagance will begin or continue. It is easy to read the stories of the Bible and allow them to touch us for a few minutes, but then close the book and shut out the message it contains. Our story, though recorded almost twenty-one centuries ago, still speaks today and has the ability, if we let it, to empower and inspire us as we live our lives in the demands of modern life. Family, jobs, dreams, deadlines, demands, disappointments, responsibilities and pain – all crowd into our heart, making survival our goal and the status quo an achievement. The thought of living extravagantly in the midst of all this is, for some, a thought too far. Yet, if we have the humility to learn from this woman and the courage to follow her example, we can make a way for the perfume of extravagance to touch His heart and enrich our lives. Though the extravagance we've spoken off is Jesus-centric, the impact of the perfume intended for Him always leaves a deposit of grace on others, even if they don't understand or like what we do.

Our English word "extravagant" comes from the Latin word *extravagari*, which means "to wander outside or beyond" from *extra* – "outside of" and *vagari* – "wander, roam". The original idea of the word carried a negative nuance, pointing to working outside prescribed lines and therefore being wasteful or reckless; thus extravagance was seen as foolish, not commendable. But as we have examined the actions of this woman, we have observed someone who was prepared to go "outside the lines" of what was accepted and expected in order to demonstrate her love and passion for Jesus. Her extravagance was perhaps wild and appalling to Simon and his friends, but it was perfectly normal to her.

Extravagance is the deliberate and intentional decision to operate outside the lines. In crossing the line we *pass the bounds of reason*, our behaviour may seem to others *wild, absurd, flamboyant, abundant or even wasteful*, but for those consumed with passion, life outside the line becomes *a new normal* and a new way of living where old boundaries are crossed and unchartered territory explored. That night, in the most unlikely of places and in the most incredible of ways, the woman took a walk on the wild side, not because she was rebellious but because she was grateful. In doing so, she created *a new normal* for herself, and now urges us to do the same!

But what takes us outside the line? What empowers us over an established practice boundary? What helps us create *a new normal*?

When we move from information to revelation
Information is helpful, but revelation is transformational. A number of years ago, I was an assistant to children with special needs in mainstream education. My job was to shadow a child (acting like a ninja was difficult when you are the only adult in the room apart from the teacher), sit with them or near

them in class and make sure they understood what was going on and had everything they needed to function effectively. I must say, I really loved it and every day was a full-on challenge. In one of our science classes the young people were learning about the dangers of smoking and were asked to watch a DVD. The presentation was brutal, showing the risks of tobacco, climaxing with a guy communicating through a hole in his throat, because cancer had eaten his voice box. However, as I looked around the room, the kids were laughing, making fun of the poor man on the screen and some of them were even publicly flashing the cigarettes they had hidden in their bags. The message wasn't getting through.

A few months ago, I met a lady in her fifties who had smoked all her life and before quitting was smoking forty cigarettes a day. I asked her why she quit so suddenly. She said she was experiencing numbness in her hands and various other parts of her body, so she went to see the doctor who told her that not only was the numbness due to smoking, but if she continued to smoke, the numbness would only get worse. She walked out of the surgery and quit!

This experience reminded me again of the difference between information and revelation. The kids in the class were being hit with information – all good, factual and necessary – but as far as they were concerned it wasn't real or relevant to them. Thus, what they saw on the screen would happen to somebody else. For the lady, the message about smoking had become real and it had hit home in the most dramatic way. She had previously known smoking was bad for her health, but now she *really knew*, and what she *really knew* changed everything!

Information is a good thing, because it informs us and if

we're wise it will push us in the right direction, but I've come to the conclusion that revelation is a better thing, because it transforms us, causing us to do by default what we may have had to do by instruction. When it comes to the world of faith and worship, this is a trap many fall into. They settle for the information route, rather than pursuing revelation. In the world of information they are told what to do, whereas in the world of revelation, they know what to do. If information alone rules, then our actions are "have to" expressions, whereas revelation transforms them into "want to" actions.

I've discovered that adoration follows appreciation. The definition of "appreciate" is "to recognise fully the worth of something" and that is not just an informational issue, rather that's a revelation. When we see it for ourselves, something changes; the value of that thing or person or purpose changes and we're not simply listening to what others have seen. I love football, but sometimes if I can't get to see it on TV, I have to listen to it on the radio. Listening to a match is an agonising experience, because one is completely reliant on the eyes of another person. The problem is, they will only relay to me what *they* see, or what they deem to be important as they see it. Therefore, my interpretation of the match and events on the pitch are completely at the mercy of what someone else is seeing and not what I'm seeing! Worship follows wonder, but I cannot worship off the wonder of another – I must wonder for myself if I am to worship with extravagance.

We'll never cross the line until we see it for ourselves. I am thankful for the information of others, but when it comes to a lifestyle of extravagance, there is no substitute for seeing it with our own eyes. We cannot worship without wonder and we'll never adore until we appreciate. Like the woman, we need to see Jesus for ourselves!

When our expectations are not framed by the experience of others

I love travelling and have had the privilege of visiting many countries of the world. Being someone who loves to plan, if I'm going anywhere new, I like to find out if any of my friends have been there and so ask their advice on what to look for or avoid. Failing that, of course, there's always the trip advisory type websites that give ratings for hotels, restaurants and experiences in that city or country. This seems like a sensible thing to do, but I've discovered it's not always helpful. Any opinion is subjective and travel is no exception. A person's view of any trip will be impacted by their expectations before the trip, their personality, the airline they flew with, the hotel they stayed in, the weather and the condition of their bags when they arrived ... if they arrived! The place may have been amazing, but their experience of it may have been horrible!

On the other hand their destination may have been pretty average, but because their expectations were low or they were just really positive people, they gave it 5 stars! On one such trip, I asked a friend who had been there previously for their opinion ... and I wish I hadn't. He spoke of terrifying border control agents, cameras in hotel rooms and a level of vigilance that might get me deported. On top of that the food wasn't very good and the climate was intolerable. I still remember that trip. It was brilliant! Sure, security was tight and the girls on reception may well have been government agents, but the food was great, the people were amazing, the beds were soft and the water was warm. Although, I did get changed in the dark just in case the cameras were on!

If we are not careful, we allow the experience of others to set the boundaries of our expectations. Had the woman behaved

Extravagant

in a pharisaic way the perfume would have stayed in the bottle, forever! Simon's experience and those of his friends, dictated that worship and religion be done a certain way, and her way was definitely not in the handbook. This is not to deny or criticise other people's experience, for as I've already said, worship follows wonder and adoration follows appreciation and we can only truly be extravagant out of the revelation we have received. However, we must not allow someone else's experience set the boundaries for our own expectations. If we do, we'll never *travel* and if we do travel, we'll only go to the places that they liked and enjoyed. Her extravagance that night was an unchartered experience for Simon and his guests, but just because he had never been there, didn't mean that she could not go! Extravagance will open our eyes to a new horizon of expectation and create a new world of experience.

When our focus is on worshipping the Lord rather than pleasing people

People possession can be a big issue, especially when it comes to areas of passion. By *people possession* I mean an unnecessary or unhealthy obsession with other people's opinions about our actions, resulting in a desire on our part to try and keep them happy. Now, it is right that we should behave with emotional intelligence and social awareness and sensitivity. There are moments when my freedom should not become a snare to others, and Paul encourages us that our generosity can at times be demonstrated in exercising our freedom to abstain.[1] However, if keeping everyone happy is at the forefront of our mind, then extravagance will never see the light of day. As we've seen through our story, extravagance will always impact and potentially divide any room, but a preoccupation with how others are going to react will ensnare our hearts and paralyse our passions. Had the woman aimed to please Simon, she would have left town, not turned up at his house.

When I fell in love with Dawn I noticed that I became less bothered with people's opinions of how I behaved towards her, and more consumed with pleasing her and doing the things she liked. Yes, of course, I took advice and behaved appropriately, especially in the context of Bible college where we enjoyed the first nine months of our relationship, but she became my obsession; she was the centre of my attention in any room … and she still is! My love for her and the demonstration of that love for her has brought me to the place were I don't really care what others think. Rather, my preoccupation is about how she feels. I want my children to see how much I love her. I want my world to know she is my Queen, and I want her to know that, apart from the Lord Himself, she is the most important person in my universe! What may look extravagant to others, has become my normal.

I have discovered that people pleasing never works, because the sort of people that need me to please them, are rarely satisfied, whatever I do. If I'm conservative then I'm boring and if I'm generous I'm over the top. If I keep quiet I've got a problem, and if I praise with exuberance I'm insensitive. If I don't take a day off I'm stupid, but when I chill out I'm lazy. If I put the church first I'm neglecting my family and if I put my family first I'm sinning against the church. I've discovered I'm never really going to win with certain types of people, so I've made a decision to lower my expectations of them, reduce the pressure on myself, and focus my primary energies on the passion of my soul. I've come to a place of intentionally not caring about what others think about my extravagance. No one apologises to me for the team they support, the holidays they take, how they spend their money or what they give their lives to ... so why should I? Jesus is the centre of my world. He has transformed my life and given me a hope and future beyond my wildest dreams. He is everything to me and all I want to do is please Him. If people like that, great, but if they don't, tough. I'm not apologising for loving Him, serving Him or giving to Him. Having been forgiven much, I'm determined to love Him much.

When generosity is about giving and not getting
Though the idea of reciprocity is a good one, I love the fact that the Kingdom gives without strings attached. When Jesus taught the people, He made reference to the normal practice of reciprocity:

"If you love those who love you, what credit is that to you?"

"And if you do good to those who are good to you, what credit is that to you?'

"And if you lend to those from whom you expect repayment, what credit is that to you?"

Note how He concluded:

"But love your enemies, do good to them, and lend to them without expecting to get anything back. Then your reward will be great, and you will be children of the Most High, because He is kind to the ungrateful and wicked. Be merciful, just as your Father is merciful."

It looks like Jesus is reinforcing reciprocity when it comes to the Kingdom, but He's actually doing the opposite. He's challenging the mentality of "safe-giving" – that is, only giving to those who will give back and only lending to those who will pay back, and He's encouraging a Kingdom mentality that gives without expectation of return, from those to whom we give. Instead, Jesus encourages His followers to give because it is the Kingdom thing to do, and leave the reward to the Lord. Later on in the same passage Jesus concludes:

"Give, and it will be given to you..."[2]

He's not contradicting Himself here, rather He's moving us from a *mindset of return* to a *culture of reward*. They sound like the same thing, but they are very different. If I give with a return mentality, then I'm expecting back whatever I gave. I scratched your back so you should scratch mine. I gave you an amount of money, I expect that amount back in return. I'm expecting something back from the context into which I gave. This is return thinking, but Jesus teaches this is not Kingdom thinking.

Rather the Kingdom thinks "reward", which radically shifts our focus when we give. When we give the Kingdom way we're giving "as unto God" (even though we might be giving to a person) and we're leaving the reward to His discretion. We're not making a financial investment, rather we're making a Kingdom deposit. When I think this way, I'm giving without strings, without conditions, without any expectation of return from the people or context into which I give. Their reaction to my gift is, in one sense, irrelevant, because I'm not expecting them to return anything to me. Instead, my gift to them is unto the Lord and anything I get back is reward from Him, not return from them. When we grasp this truth, it will transform how we see Luke 6:38, possibly the most abused verse in modern Christianity when it comes to taking offerings. Jesus wasn't talking about money, He was advocating Kingdom mentality!

If we give to get, we'll never be extravagant, because we reduce our "gift" down to a mere transaction, a financial or physical investment with a view to getting a return. When giving is just about giving, an action that is about pleasing the Lord and honouring His ways, then we cross the line, push over the border and enter a whole big world of possibility. Generosity that gives to give and not to get creates *a new normal.*

When the woman broke her bottle that night, she wasn't looking for a hundred-fold return or perhaps a down payment for a franchise in a perfume shop of her own – she just wanted to please Him, serve Him and love Him. Outside of the verbal commendation given by Jesus, we've no idea what reward she got after the conclusion of the story. She's clearly not thinking about return when she cleans and kisses His feet. She wasn't thinking return when she cracked her perfumed nard open, instead she wanted to give because giving was the right thing to do. That's what made the moment so reckless, wild and over the top, because she didn't care what she got back. She was focused only on *who* she was giving it to!

Extravagance will take us from the small world of return to the limitless world of reward. Don't give to get – *just give to give!*

When what He wants is more important than how we look
When she knelt down to serve Him that night, it was always going to look at certain way. She was a sinful woman, maybe even a prostitute, well known in the town for her sin, kneeling at the feet of Jesus acting in a less than appropriate manner towards a local Rabbi. Her actions, of course, would not only draw attention to herself, but say something about the man she was ministering to. In the culture of her day, in the context of the setting and in the emotion of the moment, it didn't look

good. But, of course, you and I know that looks can and often are deceiving. Sometimes what something looks like is what it is, but every now and again, if we only go by how it looks, we'll miss the point by a country mile!

Just ask Eli. It looked to him like Hannah was drunk, but in fact she was praying a prayer that would change her nation.[3] Just ask Michal. Her husband was shaming himself in a vulgar and unbecoming way, yet he was dancing before the Lord as His presence returned to Jerusalem.[4] Just ask Joseph. He was sure Mary had been unfaithful, but he discovered that in fact she was favoured![5] Had Hannah, David, Mary and this woman worried about how they looked, then an extravagant prayer would not have been prayed, the ark would have stayed in the house of Obed-Edom, the Angel of the Lord would have had to find another womb, and the perfume that filled the room that night may have been used for ignoble purposes! In each case, extravagance broke out because the focus was on what the Lord wanted rather than on how they looked.

We'll never create a new normal if we're worried about how it will look. Anyone who sits outside of our passion will probably misunderstand it anyway. My wife can't understand why, when I watch Liverpool on TV, I stand up to watch the game and shout at the screen. It looks weird! I struggle to comprehend why anyone would sit by a pond or river all day, trying to catch fish that, in most cases, they are going to throw back anyway. It looks weird! Turning up to a local gathering of believers on a Sunday morning when most of our neighbours are still in bed, singing at the top of our lungs, listening to the Word of God preached with passion and giving a substantial chunk of our wealth away, is hard to explain to an outsider. To them, it looks weird! *A new normal* is only forged when people stop worrying about how it looks and start enjoying it for what it is. Now, if we're doing stuff that is unnecessarily weird, then we need to address that, but if what we're doing is the expression of our passion for Him, then we'll just have to live with the weird label for a while!

John in his Gospel declares:

"The Word became flesh and made His dwelling among us..." (John 1:14)

The embodiment of the Word in flesh, the person we call Jesus, is an act of unparalleled extravagance. God so loved the world that He was prepared to cross all boundaries and explore a territory that had never, ever been explored before. When the Word entered flesh, this was new ground for everyone, and it seems on the surface of it, a bit weird, out there, over the top and unnecessary. Yet, for those who believe, for those who have moved from information to revelation, the incarnation is the very definition of extravagance itself. For the world the Lord *passed the bounds of reason,* His behaviour was *wild, absurd, flamboyant, abundant or even wasteful* ... yet, through His gift to us, we have the "right to be called children of God".

I am only able to type these words into my laptop because of *that extravagant gift.* I have the opportunity to live an eternally meaningful and hope-filled life because of *that extravagant gift.* Anything of true worth I have is because of *that extravagant gift.* To those sitting on the outside it looks like the mad act of a ridiculous God. But for those who have tasted His grace and experienced His mercy, it is the most glorious demonstration of extravagance the world will ever see. Extravagance will always look weird and unseemly to those who don't get it, but to those who do, it becomes our *new normal* and part of our every day. Don't stop at the information boundary but press on to the unexplored world of revelation. Don't allow your expectations to be framed and limited by other people's experiences, create your own. Let your focus be on worshipping the Lord and worry less about pleasing people. Give because it's good to give and not because you're hoping to get something back, and let what He wants be your motivation, for when it is, you won't be bothered about how you look.

Of the woman Jesus said:

"I tell you, her sins – and they are many – have been forgiven, *so she has shown Me much love...*"[6]

The call of extravagance is not so much about what we do, but why we do it. Her tears, hair, kisses and perfume were ultimately about one thing: demonstrating as best she could, her passionate love for Him. Her debt had been cancelled and as a result a new life had begun. His mercy and grace had created that new life for her and, as her offering demonstrated, she entered into *a new normal.*

If we love, as we've been forgiven then extravagance will be our new normal!

Endnotes

1. 1 Corinthians 8-9
2. Luke 6:27-38
3. 1 Samuel 1-2
4. 2 Samuel 6
5. Matthew 1:18-25
6. New Living Translation, my italics.

About the Author

Dr John Andrews has been in full-time church leadership since 1987, and has ministered in over 30 nations of the world with a passion to equip and inspire leaders as well as empower followers of Jesus into effective lifestyle and service.

After leaving Bible college, John helped pioneer and re-purpose a church in the village of Havercroft, West Yorkshire (1987-1997). From Havercroft he moved to Rotherham New Life in South Yorkshire (now called the Hub Christian Community), where he helped re-purpose the church into a vibrant missional community, serving from 1997-2012. In 2012 John joined the team of Renewal Christian Centre in Solihull, where he served as the Senior Associate Leader until the end of 2014. John is now the Principal of Mattersey Hall where he serves to help raise up a new generation of Christian leaders and influencers. A graduate of Mattersey, he also holds a Masters degree in Pentecostal and Charismatic Studies from Sheffield University and a Doctorate from the University of Wales. In the lecture room, he teaches "Lukan Perspectives on Mission" and "Biblical Perspectives on the Local Church".

He has authored eleven books, including *First Day – Discovering the Freedom of Sabbath-centric Living*, *2:52 – Learning to Grow on Purpose*, and *The Freedom of Limitation – Going Beyond by Staying Within*.

John is married to Dawn and together they have three children, Elaina, Simeon and Beth-Anne, not forgetting Pepperoni and Salami (the sausage dogs). John's hobbies include supporting his beloved football team, Liverpool, listening to music, reading, watching great movies, and eating great food.

www.drjohnandrews.co.uk